Poetry in Motion

Surrey Vol I

Edited by Annabel Cook

 Young**Writers**

First published in Great Britain in 2004 by:
Young Writers
Remus House
Coltsfoot Drive
Peterborough
PE2 9JX
Telephone: 01733 890066
Website: www.youngwriters.co.uk

SB ISBN 1 84460 411 X

Foreword

This year, the Young Writers' 'Poetry In Motion' competition proudly presents a showcase of the best poetic talent selected from over 40,000 up-and-coming writers nationwide.

Young Writers was established in 1991 to promote the reading and writing of poetry within schools and to the youth of today. Our books nurture and inspire confidence in the ability of young writers and provide a snapshot of poems written in schools and at home by budding poets of the future.

The thought effort, imagination and hard work put into each poem impressed us all and the task of selecting poems was a difficult but nevertheless enjoyable experience.

We hope you are as pleased as we are with the final selection and that you and your family continue to be entertained with *Poetry In Motion Surrey Vol I* for many years to come.

Contents

Blenheim High School

Sam Kilpatrick (11)	65
Jake Phillp (11)	65
Hannah Vincent (11)	66
Lucy Pidgeon (11)	66
Jack Wood (11)	67
Jessica Ramsey (11)	67
Stephen Pryce (11)	67
Jordan Fitzpatrick (11)	68
Naomi Waters (12)	68
Deena Ahmed (11)	68
Adam Keehn (11)	69
Natasha Bayley (11)	69
Tiffany Wayman (11)	70
Max Robinson (11)	70
Naomi Snelling (11)	71
Becky Hindle (12)	71
Kim Bartram (11)	71
Alice Hoy (11)	72
Sean Harris (11)	72
Nazia Sooruth (13)	73
Harry McKeown (11)	73
Sam Swindells (11)	74
Sarah Lyon (11)	74
Steve Baker (11)	74
Courtney Barella (11)	75
Daniel Wright (11)	75
Francesca Nott (11)	75
Hannah Conibeer (11)	76
Ben Hodgkins (11)	76
Amy Housego (11)	77
Alex Hale (11)	77
Maddie Cooper (11)	78
Harry Rodd (11)	78
Aaron Johnson (12)	79
Callum Wilkinson (11)	79
Oliver Gaynor (11)	80
Tristan White (11)	80
Harriett Church Jennings (11)	80
George Parnell (12)	81
Joshua Beecher (11)	81
Sophie Owen (11)	81
Ashleigh Bruen (11)	82

Hannah Kraushaar (11) 82
Lucy Smith (11) 82
Samantha Henry (11) 83
Elliot Draper (11) 83
Christie Grimwood (11) 83
Ryan Jordan (11) 84
Dean Sale (11) 84
Sean Starkey (12) 84
Geoffrey Sparham (11) 85
Kirstie Locke (11) 85

Esher CE High School
Amberley Self (12) 85
Louis Whittle (14) 86
Katie Ovington (15) 87
Ella Smith (15) 88
Hannah Slatter (12) 89

Kingston Grammar School
Greg Whitby (11) 89
Oliver Woodings (11) 90
Ben Kumar (14) 90
Michael Stenning (12) 91
Katie O'Neill (14) 91
Sarika Rice (12) 92
Alex Grounds (13) 92
Kabir Sandhu (12) 93
Aimée Connolly (12) 93
Geraldine Evans (13) 94
Laurence Todd (14) 95
Susanna Goffe (12) 95
Andrew Chan (14) 96
Calum Smith (14) 97
Lottie Naughton-Rumbo (14) 98
Nicola Gale (13) 98
Zoë Handrill (15) 99
Rosalind Axbey (12) 99
Nikhil-Raj McDuff (14) 100
Thomas Osborne (14) 100
Huw Procter (14) 101
Abigail King (13) 102

St Philomena's School, Carshalton

The Poems

The Night She Died

Great and bold,
The steel so cold,

Rich and poor,
Pets galore,

Grand and good,
First class could,

Take the chance,
And dance,

The plates gleamed,
In the steam,

There it was hard to see,
She tried to flee,
Couldn't succeed,

Water came,
Waters fame,

Lives gone,
Some lives shone,

Now it's gone,
Forever gone,

The sea's prize,
Cost many lives,

The Titanic gone in 2 hours,
The graves covered in flowers,

Many years an enquiry goes on,
Was it all a con?

Chloe Cox (11)

In That Box

Look it's David Blaine, see him.
I wonder what he is doing
Is he mad or what?
No, he's staying in that glass box.

How long is he staying there?
44 days and nights without washing his hair
When he comes out he will look disgusting
But he's doing it for his fans who love him.

Oh no, he's not allowed to eat
He's missing his favourite meal, chips and meat
But what's this, no that's not fair
A cheese burger hanging down from the air.

What's next, nothing, it's all quiet
Good because I don't want a riot
Oh damn, it's happened now
Splat a paintball, just before the night.

George Roff (10)

Looking Further Than The Eyes

What do you see when you look at me?
An innocent girl of just 14?
An angry face with sharp-looking eyes?
Eyes that know nothing or eyes that are wise?
Do you see trouble or do you see strife?
A girl going nowhere making waste of her life?
Do you see tension? I might be afraid,
a troublesome path of what has been made.
Do you see happiness, a girl without stress
that always lives life coming out best?
Whose world is at ease from what's going on,
oblivious of pain and of what's going wrong?
So many things may pass through my mind,
some are remembered and some left behind.
So when you've worked out what you see inside me,
try to remember I'm a girl of 14!

Lucy Parkes (14)

Friends

What memories we'll have my friend
When we are old and grey
We've laughed and cried
We've screamed and sighed,
Every night and every day we'll tell our tales
Of our adventures while wide-eyed
Grandchildren stare at our dentures
Our walking sticks
Will stand together
As we begin
Our last adventure.

Emma Watts (11)
Bishopsford Community School

Let Me Be

Why do you think it rains
When you feel sad?
Why do you think it rains
When you feel lonely?
Why do you think it rains
When you feel like no one cares?
Why do you think it rains at all?

Why do you think it rains
When you are heartbroken?
Why do you think it rains
When you are down?
Why do you think it rains
When you are foreign?
Why do you think it rains at all?
You deserve to be happy
That way the sun can shine . . .

Kylie Botchway (15)
Bishopsford Community School

The Wind, The Wind

The wind, the wind
flows through the air.

The wind, the wind
goes everywhere.

The wind, the wind
blows through my hair.

The wind, the wind
runs through with no care.

The wind, the wind . . .

David Kelly (12)
Bishopsford Community School

The Sea

The sea,
The mermaid's home,
Glittering and glistening
In the morning sun.

The sea,
The beautiful sea,
The waves racing
And the seaweed swaying.

The sea,
Like a painted picture,
A never-ending tub of water,
On which the sun shines
Like a golden pathway.

The sea,
Home of the creatures,
That swim in the moonlights.

The sea,
With the tiny fairies,
That skip along the navy blanket.

The sea,
What a beautiful thing,
Soothing and calming
With the cool, fresh breeze.

Kira Watchorn (12)
Bishopsford Community School

Rushing Wind

The wind is blowing me all around,
The wind makes a howling sound,
Blow me left, blow me right,
Blow me like it wants to fight.

The wind is freezing, the wind is cold,
The wind is evil I've been told,
It was once hot but now it's not,
The wind is bold, that means it's cold.

Thunder and lightning is a fright,
It blows up like dynamite,
I never knew what it could do,
It could kill me or it could kill you.

Rushing wind from here to there,
Rushing wind everywhere,
Left, right, centre, through the trees,
The wind shall enter.

Parise Wong (13)
Bishopsford Community School

Crash And Burn

Burnt face,
Upset and misplace
Rough and sore
Nasty and poor
Tears trickling down
This burnt face
Memories in this place
Crash and burn.

Kira Bellinger (13)
Bishopsford Community School

Me!

I am who I am,
No one can change that,
I am myself,
But I may be different,
I am who I am,
I'm not someone else,
I'm me.

I may not like music,
I may not like maths,
I may, I may not,
But I am myself,
Not anyone else.

I have to be myself,
Or I wouldn't be me,
I am happy who I am,
Because that's me.

I'm me and only me!

Shelley Redgrave (13)
Bishopsford Community School

Burns

Burns are ugly,
Burns are sore.
Burns are painful,
Burns galore.

Everyone stares and talks
But no one knows
The painful feeling,
That burns are ugly,
Burns are sore.

Fern Fay (13)
Bishopsford Community School

Womanhood

It's when a girl becomes a woman
It's when their style and personality changes
It's when they start getting interested in boys
And get involved with love and games.

It's when they start getting moody and want stuff their way
It's when their dad gets overprotective about the boys they date
It's when they start to worry more about how they look,
Their make-up and their hair
It's when they start to go out with their friends all the time
Go out to the malls and buy, buy, buy

It's not as simple as childhood used to be,
Happy, nice and free
Womanhood is complicated,
It's about growing as a person in style and personality.

Skye Seery (14)
Bishopsford Community School

The Crash

He didn't know about the car until they went too far
Smash! Bash! Crash! Went the vehicle
He survived, now that was a miracle
But his face was really burnt,
That was a lesson that he learnt.

In hospital he lay and cried
He was groaning and moaning and opened his eyes
His mum and dad said their hellos and goodbyes
He was shocked as he looked in the mirror
Then he lay down on his painful pillow.

Scott Brockwell (13)
Bishopsford Community School

Justice And Law

Justice
Why are many people addicted to you?
Is it because you are fair?
Why do people prefer you to law?
Is it because the truth comes out?
Why do people rely so much on you?
Is it because you bring out the truth?
Why do people run to you?
Is it because you set them free?
Why do people praise you?
Is it because of your faithfulness?
Oh justice!

Law
Why are many people rejecting you?
Is it because you are unfair?
Why do people prefer justice to you?
Is it because the truth doesn't come out?
Why don't people rely on you at all?
Is it because you are annoying?
Why don't people run to you?
Is it because you don't set them free?

Derrick Boansi (14)
Bishopsford Community School

The Sea

The sea is another word for the ocean,
The ocean blows in the wind's direction,
You feel the spray of the water,
It splashes you lightly from head to toe,
The sea is so windy and wavy,
The waves are like a big tiger's roar,
But on a summer's day
The sea stays still as if waves don't exist.

Natasha Rouse (12)
Bishopsford Community School

Racism And Discrimination

Black or white what does it matter?
The black are poor, the white are better.
Discrimination is near you all day long,
But is it right or is it wrong?

People are fighting all over the place,
If it isn't for power then it's about other people's race.
Why can't people normally work together?
If that would happen the world would be a lot better.

Why isn't there peace between black and white?
What is going on now just isn't right!
If people all were the same,
Then there isn't a different race they can blame.

Shouting, swearing and fighting
What in the world is happening?
All humans are exactly the same,
But why do they still give each other the blame?

Imagine all the people were good friends,
All the discrimination and racism will maybe ends!

Dennis Vermeulen (13)
Bishopsford Community School

Surviving In The Jungle . . .

Surviving in the jungle is a scary thing to do,
Surviving in the jungle without any drink or food.
Surviving in the jungle sleeping amongst the apes and trees,
Surviving in the jungle with all the insects and fleas.
Surviving in the jungle without the telly,
Surviving in the jungle you would be rather smelly.
Surviving in the jungle without a friend or two,
Surviving in the jungle needing to go to a loo.
Surviving in the jungle in the dark and cold,
Surviving in the jungle wouldn't be very bold.

Coran Gough (12)
Bishopsford Community School

Racism

It doesn't matter about the colour of the skin.
All that matters is what's within.

But people take this differently,
They can only judge about what they can see.

They do no wrong and are treated like slaves
Only because they are a different race.

The fear, the anger is what takes place
Causing sudden death or suicide.

The soul and spirit must carry on
For a person who has done no wrong.

But for a racist their soul is destroyed
Because they've made the whole world annoyed.

The world is a better place
Without all this fuss about race.

All that matters is what's inside
So coloured people should have some pride.

Leanne Sleeman (13)
Bishopsford Community School

Survival Poem

It's hard on this island, working all day,
As hard as we can,
Getting up early, going to sleep late.
People getting wounded
Us trying to heal them before the day is over.
It is hard to get the fire started,
The food isn't as nice as the food that we have at home.
We are all waiting for the day when we can go home,
It's getting late, time to go to sleep . . . zzzzzz.

Amy Harris (11)
Bishopsford Community School

Justice And Law

When a robber robs a bank,
They set off the alarms.
The police then come running
And they all get disarmed.

They are taken to the police station,
In a Black Maria.
They get chucked in a cell,
To await their trial.

They are then taken to court,
To face the judge.
They then plead their case,
With an ashen looking face.

They then get their sentence,
Which is not very good.
They've now learnt their lesson,
They will be good now on.

The lesson to be learnt from this,
Is if you break the law,
Justice will be served
And you'll get what you deserve.

Cassie Melbourne (14)
Bishopsford Community School

Black And Proud

I may be different
I may be black

You hit me
And I hit back

But that's no reason
To act as you do

So I say out loud
I'm black and proud.

Chloe Greenfield (14)
Bishopsford Community School

Untitled

It bites and tears even to the spirit of its victims.
It savagely and unmercifully rips open wounds,
Not to heal, but to put salt, then poison in.
It laps up great pleasure from other mortals suffering,
It thrives on it.
The pain is so agonising it comes in the form of dreams
Or thought to haunt many depressed souls.
'He's gone, I'll be next.' 'Many have gone south,'
'It'll be my turn soon.' or 'It's about time I joined 'em.'
All churning over and over and over
Till it's driven into oblivion, taking with it all sanity,
All hope, all logic, care, calmness, love,
Everything that's needed in this world to live.
That's the meaning of 'trench' only by half.
Desperate, starved corpses that's what they were.
Those 'poor, poor men'.

Heather Smith
Bishopsford Community School

I Have To Stand

Here I stand at the front of the bus,
I stand here quietly, not making a fuss.
There are seats at the back,
But they are not for blacks.
If I was white I would have a seat,
But as I'm black, I have to nurse my aching feet.
If I did sit at the back,
I know my eyes will go black,
So I stand here at the front of the bus,
I stand here quietly, not making a fuss.

Simon Rosser (14)
Bishopsford Community School

We Are Equal

I was put in jail,
I wonder why I'm here!
I beat up a black man,
And left him lying there!
I know I shouldn't have done it,
I know he's just like me!
The only difference is
He looks different to me!
I don't know why I did it,
But now I'm stuck in here!
I am such a coward,
To leave him lying there!
I thought he might have made it,
But now he is in Heaven!
Or at least I hope he is, but me,
I'm stuck in here - just where I ought to be!

Emma Harding (13)
Bishopsford Community School

The Sea

It's so big and white,
As deep as the earth,
Some fish have never been seen,
Some parts are as deep as space itself
Still places never been.

It joins countries around the world,
Places I long to be.
This weird and wonderful scary thing
That's called the deep blue sea.

Kieron Foley (13)
Bishopsford Community School

Max's Unexpected Death

15 lucky students from Fleetwood
went on a journey one day
they went to Red Tarn Beck
in the spring month of May.

They went with Mr Ellis
and Mrs Palmer too
Mr Ellis wanted a diving competition
which she also wanted to do.

The mud was soggy on the banks
the water was extremely cold
the teacher said it was alright
so they did what they were told.

Max jumped in second
'cause he thought it would be alright
until he found in the water
that his muscles became all tight.

He couldn't move much
his mum gave a worrying frown
she did know what to do
but she didn't think he'd drown.

Mr Ellis jumped in after him
but didn't think anything would go wrong
he tried to save him but couldn't
so his death was horribly long.

Max's body was found
his mum let out a tear
Mr Ellis was a worried man
but didn't think he would get jailed for a year.

Simon Graham (12)
Bishopsford Community School

A Ship And The Sea

Long, long ago on a bright and breezy day,
A wooden old ship named The Core set sail,
Hoist the sail we're off to sea, begin the feast,
The sun was shining brightly among a tail.

The mist green tail sunk down while the head arose,
'Sea creature, sea creature!' they shout about,
Captain fired his crossbow at the green beast,
The beast dived down, which rocked the boat about.

They spotted a nearby, old rocky dark cave,
So they sailed for hideout from the beast,
There they waited, quiet in sound, till nightfall,
As night had fallen they set sail south-east.

As they began to set sail a storm brewed,
'Get below decks,' the captain started to shout,
The storm was fierce, but soon calmed itself down,
The sun rose at dawn over a whale's spout.

Whilst sailing along seas, dolphins came to join,
The pirates and crew fed the dolphins fish,
Mary Boo the cook nearly had dinner done,
Around the table pirates liked their dish.

Night fell, the pirates went to their cosy hammocks,
The pirates snored as the wind blew all night,
Before the sun awoke, pirates cleaned the decks,
The morning sun arose, shining full bright.

'Land ahoy, straight ahead,' the captain ordered,
'Hooray, hooray,' the crew began to yell,
We're home at last, grab the anchor for ashore,
The captain said our story we shall sell.

Christine Sturt (12)
Bishopsford Community School

Geoffrey Chaucer And The Canterbury Tales

Sitting in my room late one night,
Pen to paper; a poem, I had to write.
About Geoffrey Chaucer, that was his name,
The Canterbury Tales was his claim to fame.

Twenty-four stories rolled into one,
A masterpiece in Middle English had begun.
And so, a band of pilgrims was to be the cast,
The framework, a pilgrimage, that was to be the task.

At the Tabard Inn, their journey, it did start,
Passing time, telling stories, each that came from the heart.
The Miller, the Friar, the Merchant, to name but a few,
The Physician, the Squire and the Pardoner too.

Their stories passed many hours, their journey was so long,
Each telling a tale that was better than a song.
Day turned into night, nights turned into days,
Their stories kept coming as they went on their merry way.

The Poet listened attentively as the stories they were told,
The Clerk, Cook, Knight and Shipman's stories rolled,
Off these pilgrim's tongues, it was better than a feast!
With the Monk, Franklin, Man of Law, Miller and Nun's Priest!

Canterbury at last! For this strange-looking bunch
Had decided that for the best story the rest would buy a lunch!
It had taken many a long night and day
But all had heard and told new wonders along the way.

And so my tale is told, in this my late night poem,
I hope you like it and a feast for me might now be owing!
One day, like Chaucer, my poems might be on sale too!
You never know, it might just be a tale for you!

Jenner Richardson (12)
Bishopsford Community School

About Us People

Love is blind, love is cold
Why are we different colours, I will never be told
Me and you, we are one
Together we have lots of fun.

What is love if it can't be found?
All the earth is big and round.
Everyone is the same but only in other ways,
People have had some special days.

Black or white, tiny or tall,
People shouldn't be taken for a fool
Up above, down below
Everyone shouts hello.

Amy-Louise Garner (13)
Bishopsford Community School

Manliness

The one who's manly
is the one that's brave!
The one who's not
hides in a cave.

The one who's manly
doesn't tell a lie.
The one who's not
sits there and cries.

The one who's manly
is not a coward.
The one who's not
is a . . .

Dardan Meholli (15)
Bishopsford Community School

Racism

What is black?
What is white?
We're all the same in my heart
There is no difference between us.

Love black
Love white
You'll never know who is right
There is no difference between us.

Black is a colour
White is a colour
We are not different from each other.

Being black
Or being white,
It's not wrong, it's not right.

Love every colour
Let every colour love you
We are not different from one another.

Every colour can love
Every colour has a heart
There is no difference between us.

Am I black?
Am I white?
It's just the same in my heart
There is no difference between us.

Someone tell me what is racism?
And why are we racist to one another
Even though we are not different from each other?

James Matlock (13)
Bishopsford Community School

Judgmental

The colour of our skin
separates us from each other,
no matter what our colour
we are all equal and free.

We have no control
over what others think of us,
but we can choose
what we think and see in others,
we can choose our actions.

There is good, bad and evil in all,
but you can never see
what a person is by just looking at them.
Appearances cannot tell us
everything or anything sometimes.
Don't judge a book by its cover.

Emma Todd (13)
Bishopsford Community School

Everyone Is Equal

People being killed
racism to blame
everyone is equal,
so don't treat each other
any other way.

Just try and get along
or this world might split in two
if not for yourself then
for someone close to you.

Hannah Nye (13)
Bishopsford Community School

How Much I Love You!

I love you . . .
Like the rose loves its petals,
Like the grass loves the mud,
Like the sun loves the sky,
Like the paint loves the brush,
Like my mum loves my dad,
Like the teacher loves her work,
Like the kids love to chat,
Like the heart loves the liver,
Like the eye loves the tear,
Like the sea loves the sand,
Like the bird loves its wings,
Like the paper loves the pen,
That's how much I love you!

Clarissa Lecras (12)
Bishopsford Community School

Racism

Why do people show such hate
Being offensive to others in this state?
Whether you're American, Spanish, Jamaican
Black, white, German or Asian.

In the end we should all be equal
And not carry on another sequel.
When the next generation grow old
Maybe people won't be so cold.

One day racism will leave us in peace
So discrimination will cease.
Hopefully this poem has brought some sense
Into this present tense.

Nathan Burke (13)
Bishopsford Community School

End Prejudice

E vil, nasty words spoken to hurt the unique
N ine terrible letters which spell out p-r-e-j-u-d-i-c-e
D isasterous riots, protests and even suicide
   caused by all this nonsense.

P rejudice is an evil thing.
R acism against unique people.
E nvy and hate, where is the peace?
J udging people for looks.
U nderstand that people are all equal.
D ifferent from others and left alone
I nside a person's feelings are hurt.
C reates a war between different people.
E nd this battle of hate and fear,
   Why can't we all just get alone?

Henna Mian (13)
Bishopsford Community School

Black And White

We should all be treated the same.

B eware of racism
L et it be a thing we shouldn't discuss
A nd can't hear from someone's mouth
C rying for acceptance to whites
K eep racism hidden from everyone.

&

W hite and black should be together!
H atred in this world has a collection
I n everyone there's a heart
T he skin shouldn't have to matter
E veryone just have peace and love.

Leah Wright (13)
Bishopsford Community School

Weather Days

Rainy days are pouring, rainy days are wet.
Tuesdays are the worst days 'cause homework's always set.

Rainy days make puddles on the ground and greens.
Sunny days are great 'cause the sun shows its golden beams.

Icy days are chilly, frost hardens the ground
In the moors of Epsom you can hear its cracking sound.

Snowy days are better than all this put together
As we dress the snowman in his orange sweater.

Victoria Hall (12)
Bishopsford Community School

Racism

Don't judge me by the colour of my skin
Judge by what is within.
Don't judge me by the way I talk
We should be close like a board and chalk.
Don't judge me by the way I stand,
Blacks and whites should come hand in hand.
So judge me by the way I am created
Judge me with love and not with hatred.

Michael Mogbo-Peters (13)
Bishopsford Community School

Racism

R ight or wrong?
A cting or judging people because they're different
    why has it been going on for so long?
C reating pain for others, it's not right.
I njuring others by their skin colour, that's so tight.
S ome die, some live in terrible nightmare.
M ost people used to be racists but nowadays it's rare.

Decca Omar (13)
Bishopsford Community School

No Matter What

Everybody should be treated the same,
The fact they're not it is a shame.
Everybody should have the same rights
And not be shouting and getting into fights.

Black, white, English or not
People are the same no matter what.
People hurt, people dying
Children are the ones left crying.

God made the world big and round
So we can be together safe and sound.
We should be able to get on
And live in this world together as one.

Claire Carter (13)
Bishopsford Community School

Racist Poem

Colour is such a big thing.
I can't understand why there is all this fuss.
All over skin colour,
Which does not change a person's feelings or personality.
People's lives lost every day, all over skin colour.
People crying, all over skin colour.
People hurt, all over skin colour.
When will there be equality between skin colours?
Think of the kids of a whole new world.
Why make their lives a misery?
Why?

Jade Lovegrove (13)
Bishopsford Community School

Untitled

Out of sight, out of place
In this place and time
My world is moving round
Nowhere for comfort or peace
Draw me closer
I feel pain in my heart
I beg you not to let me go
In this time and place
I want you to hold me
Wishes may come true
Dreams could keep on dreaming
But they are nothing compared
To the memory of you
Shattering pieces are left when you
Are not around to be there in my heart
Suffering for your love has left me feeling weak
Just one more touch of you could be a lifetime for me
Disasters have grown
Days I have spent to moan and groan
Nights I have spent crying to sleep
I just want you to be there
Please just come back to me.

Angel Ajidahun (15)
Bishopsford Community School

Face

F lames up in the air
   all you can feel is fear.
A nd all you can feel
   is a warm fearful tear.
C hanging your life
   always in pain.
E ven the memory of the crash
   when you go down that lane.

Hayley Downes (13)
Bishopsford Community School

Detention

Silence
The clock ticking away
I'm sure it doesn't work
It shouldn't be so slow.

The heat of the light above me
A drop of sweat trickled down my forehead
Tickling for a moment
Then falling, lost in a sea of black jumper.

Slowly people left
Until the room was practically empty
Brring!

I shot out of the classroom
Faster than a gun.
Free at last!

Maa-Yarkor Addo (12)
Bishopsford Community School

Face

I sit here in the corner,
Staring at the wall, staring there,
Wondering when somebody will call
Alone and scared
And I am in fear,
I hope you are coming
'Cause I need someone here.

  B eing here on my own
  U nder a lot of pressure
  R ealising what a
  N erd I really am
  T errified of my life ahead.

Gemma Dark (13)
Bishopsford Community School

The Dreams Of A Shipwreck

In the middle of the Atlantic Ocean
There lies a ship that's old,
On it is a young woman and a skeleton
The anchor in the seabed, caked with mould.

The pretty young woman is rolling some dice
Whilst her face is white and pale,
She remembers her life from the past
When the ship was set to sail.

The skeleton sits upon the mast
In its hand, an old treasure map,
Wearing a worn and tattered old cloak
Ripped and torn, mainly on the lap.

As the woman rolled her dice
She heard a tumble behind her,
There were some dead men
Each collapsing on top of each other.

There's an axe in the middle of the floor
Maybe some committed suicide,
The axe is wooden and very sharp,
Hopefully no one fell in with the tide.

The young woman hears a noise,
It's squawking, she looks to the sky,
What does she see? Only an albatross
As white as snow, flying higher than high.

Frantically she looks to sea,
To find coming towards her, a wooden boat.
Maybe the albatross was a sign, but for what?
'I'm seriously surprised that boat's still afloat!'

Emma Dickinson (12)
Bishopsford Community School

River Raging

We are here at Red Tarn Beck, where the river flows like magic,
A group of people soon arrive, shortly to be in a panic.

A teacher, a mother and 15 children, strolled up in early May,
But beware the current's strong, they're sure to have their way.

It just so happens the teacher enters, disappointed though he is,
He's frozen but lies to them, 'Come in kids.'

But bear in mind this river, those in sense would have left,
But they stayed and grew excited, before a fatal death.

So Max got undressed, ran and took a leap,
In seconds flat he was as cold as ice
And swallowed by waters deep.

He begs for help, his loving mother jumps in,
As it were the waves ate her, currents too powerful to swim.

Before you know she's asleep, Max screams, 'Don't let me die,'
His mother is saved, she awakens and cries.

Max's body rushes on, and like a frightened cat it fled,
Later found on the banks, battered, floating . . . dead.

A battle he fought, this day was meant to be fun,
This day would be remembered, Red Tarn Beck's river had won.

And so, later in court, they listened to what the other had to say,
Mother vs Teacher, what a tragic day.

In the end 12 months was given to the fool,
This cut the parents' spirits like a knife,
Just one year he had to pay, the parents would suffer for life.

Craig Smith (12)
Bishopsford Community School

The Pirate From The Caribbean

It was on a glorious morning we set the sail,
The decks were scrubbed and squeaky clean.
And if you spied, high into the sunlit sky,
There was not a cloud to be seen.

'Ahoy there!' A fearful voice rang out!
'Pirates! Pirates! All around to see!
Prepare yourselves for bloody battle!
Be brave! Me hearties!' The captain said to me.

We filled our cannons full to the brim with powdered shot
And then we fired at will
The pirates clambered aboard our ship
Then started to cunningly kill.

The pirates all had flaming torches
They burned and blazed the mast.
The fire raged through the bottom deck
And then there was a blast.

The pirates and all the crew
Were floating in the sea, quite dead.
The sharks swiftly swam in hunger
Until the sharks were fed.

I woke up from my slumber
And found myself in the salty sand.
I got up and looked around
And I saw a distant land.

Dario Diaz (11)
Bishopsford Community School

Sonnet

Does he love me or doesn't he love me?
Today he did say that I make great tea.
But he's so nice, he'd say that anyway.
So what else has he said that's good about me?
He probably likes me as a great friend,
But I want him to like me more than that.
But if my love for him comes to an end,
What would be the point of all that thinking?
What does he think of me? I still don't know.
Why can't he just come to me and tell me?
Why is he that hard to be forgotten?
Maybe he does not even think of me.
Now I'm back to square one, does he like me?
I don't think he loves me, end of thoughts.

Naima Khalid (15)
Bishopsford Community School

I Love You So Much!

I love you
I love you
I love you so much
If I were a rabbit I'd give you my hutch
If I were a bird I'd give you a tweet
If I were a child I'd give you my sweet
If I were a dog I'd give you a bone
If I were a mum I'd give you a moan
If I were a sea I'd save you a shell
If I were a phone I'd give you a bell
If I were a baby I'd give you my cot
If I were an egg I'd give up my spot
Just for you
That's how much I really love you!

Charlet Wilson (12)
Bishopsford Community School

RIP Max

A special outing
It was meant to be
Everybody was excited
But one paid a fee

It just so happened
It was with his life
He could have grown up
And had a wife

The teacher jumped in
And asked them to follow
Max jumped in
And had a lot to swallow

As he reached the water
He began to panic
His mum stood watching
She was really frantic

He screamed and screamed
Don't let me die
His mum said don't worry
It's all a lie

A team of kids
Tried to rescue him
His mum jumped in
And damaged her limb

For now you see
He has gone to a better place
His mum turned him over
And kissed his face.

Rez Mellor (12)
Bishopsford Community School

Locked In!

As the sun disappears into the dark blue sky
The graveyard turns pitch-black.
The old, broken gravestones shine in the night.
Pure silence surrounds me.
White mist creeps around my feet.
I feel lonely and scared.
Rustling trees follow me as I run,
Their branches, like skeleton's hands
Reaching out to grab me.
I hear howling from a distance.
I can barely see through the thick white mist.
The full moon shines brightly above me.
The howling's getting louder,
It's getting closer and closer.
Suddenly something grabs my trembling shoulders
Argh!

Christopher Smith (12)
Bishopsford Community School

Horror

Horror is a scary movie,
Too scared to close your eyes.
Horror is the edge of a knife,
Able to cut and slice you.
Horror is the night,
Quiet and unable to see.
Horror is all things unimaginable,
Waiting to scare you out of your skin.
It will take you by the neck and eat you alive.
Horror's a creepy thing.

Jay Seery (12)
Bishopsford Community School

Womanhood

Womanhood is hard,
when we go through so many changes,
but we still put on brave faces.

Yes we have bad tempers,
that's because men don't understand us,
but we lay down and have their babies
so what do they expect
with our hormones going crazy.

We watch our children grow
but then when they are older it's hard to let go,
we wish we could pick them off the wrong track
and wrap them up in our back packs.

It's hard for all females young or old,
and hard to be ourselves
and not what the world would like to mould.

We remember the good times
but must learn to forget the bad,
putting on a brave face when we are happy or sad.

Teach your man to love you for how you feel,
not just for the six o'clock meal,
because love doesn't come as a deal.

So men make no mistake, true love you cannot fake,
do not take us for granted,
for if you do the seed of evil will be planted.

Fight for what you think is right
because womanhood is not to be taken light.

Natasha Barnes (14)
Bishopsford Community School

What's Black Anyway?

'Why can't I go out and play?'
Sally asked her mum.
'Because she's trouble,
She's dirty . . .
She's different . . .
She's black!'

'Why won't Sally's mum let us play?'
Jenny asked her mum.
'Because she's ignorant of our kind.
All she sees is our colour.'

'But Jenny's my best friend,'
Sally told her mum.
'I always play with her at school.
She's funny, she's kind
And what's black anyway?'

Ellen Burrage (13)
Bishopsford Community School

I Love You!

If I was a cat I'd share my fish with you,
If I was a heart I would devote it to you.

I will love you till the day I die,
My love will never end, this is no lie,
I love you like a pig loves his food,
I love you like a river loves his flood.

My love and my heart will never fade,
I love you like a bucket loves its spade,
The kisses I spread I spread to you,
I love you, I love you, I love you so much.

Rosemarie Marle (12)
Bishopsford Community School

Love

Love is but something no man can describe
Not about beauty but what is inside
The feelings and hopes you share and you show
Love is inside you have just got to know
That love's not so easy like life in itself
The more that you love the less it will help.

My love for another now truly hurts
This pain that I feel is worse than I show
But how can I tell the cause of my pain
When it just causes exactly the same?
Maybe I'm wrong but I hope that it would
It would just prove that they care as I do

Love is but something no man can describe
Not about beauty but what is inside.

Jason Jacques (16)
Bishopsford Community School

How Much Do I Love You

I'll love you forever 'til the day that I die,
If I were a spider I'd give you my fly.
I love you so much, like a mum loves a daughter,
If I were a fish I'd give you my water.
I love you so much that I'd sacrifice my life,
If I were a fork I'd want you to be my knife.
I love you that much, like my hair loves gel,
If I were the sea I'd save you my shell.
I love you, I love you, I really love you.
I love you so much and I want you to love me too.

Daryl Pengelly (12)
Bishopsford Community School

The Gremlin

A gremlin is an evil creature,
It will eat a child or even a teacher,
It will follow you home very freakily,
It shall devour your guts extremely freakishly,
It will rip out your heart, just for a start,
It has 666 printed on its forehead,
Its teeth are sharp, poisonous as lead,
One night you'll be in for a fright,
It'll come to your bed and give you a bite.

Robert Singh-Staplehurst (11)
Bishopsford Community School

The Hummingbird

Hummingbird, you are so small,
Don't you get tired at all?
Flitting from flower to flower,
Drinking their sweet nectar,
Hour after hour after hour.
Hummingbird all you do is feed,
Flapping tiny wings at such a speed,
You have no time to stop and rest,
For you have babies back at the nest.

Aimee Clements (12)
Bishopsford Community School

Friendship

Friends are angels
That came from above
Sent by God for me to love
So if you're down
And not sure what to do
Just remember
I'll always be here for you.

Verneesha Alexander (11)
Bishopsford Community School

Womanhood Poem

Women have not got rights,
We now put up a very good fight.
We can be whatever we want to be.

We come in all shapes and sizes,
All colours and nationalities.

We have good days, bad and fat days
But we still have to plod along
And keep our beds made.

We give birth like it's no trouble
Because we don't want to burst our family bubble.

We are granddaughters, grandmothers,
Daughters and wives.

That's enough said
We're simply the best!

Carlene Humphries (14)
Bishopsford Community School

Manliness

A man needs to show that he is big.
A man can never let himself get put down.
A man should not be afraid.
A man should always be big.
A man doesn't cry over small things.
A man isn't emotional.
A man keeps all his true feelings to himself.
A man is strong.
A man isn't weak.

Tousif Iqbal (14)
Bishopsford Community School

The Lost Widow

As she lies on the gloomy deck
Her heart ticks in the sun.
Her mind is going potty
As she pictures soldiers on the run.

Her neck goes all funny
Arms go and give way
As she lays on the floor
Will she manage to stay?

The ship has no one
Just she who has no name
The ship protects
From she who has no shame.

Now the animals are in close
Her mind seeing a boat,
Coming her way
And looks afloat.

As they go away
Heading towards the sand
She just sitting there
Feeling like a brass band.

Mitchell Roots (13)
Bishopsford Community School

Coming Of Age

When a girl's growing up she starts to mature,
She becomes interested in boys, clothes, music and more.
Their dads always protect them wherever they go,
If they want a boyfriend and Dad always says no.
Girls always like to wear make-up and make themselves look good,
But when they have hormones they get into a mood.
Girls sometimes worry about how they are,
But now they've grown up they've got quite far.

Alex Gater (14)
Bishopsford Community School

Whispers In The Wind

The rain it said, 'How do you do?'
The wind it said, 'Hello!'
You cannot hear this,
That I know,
It is a whisper in the wind!

As the boats sailed into dock,
When the clocks struck 9 o'clock,
The wind whispered to the men,
'I will take you home again!'

As the morning sunshine came
The harbour boats were gone again.
The wind was nowhere to be seen,
And no trace he'd ever been.

Lauren Knowelden (14)
Bishopsford Community School

How Much Do I Love You

I love you . . .

Like the fish loves the sea,
Like a biscuit loves tea,
Like the sun loves the sky,
Like Jack Horner loves pie,
Like the waves love the sand,
Like the arm loves the hand,
Like the grass loves the mud,
Like vampires love blood,
Like the foot loves the shoe,
Like a cow loves its moo . . .

That's how much I love you!

Natalie Harris (12)
Bishopsford Community School

Nature Poem

In the garden at night, it's raining hard,
With drops of water dripping on leaves.
The drops glisten against the moonlit sky.
The sky turns from blue to red,
Then orange as it turns into day.
The leaves are as green as the grass,
The flowers white, red, orange and pink.
The flowers are lilies, roses, carnations and daffodils.

In the day, the bright colours of the garden
Are enhanced by the bees and shining orange sun,
Showing pinks, reds, oranges, whites and greens.
The garden smells of the flowers and the bees are collecting pollen.
The bees stand out clearly with their black and yellow stripes.
The sound of the bees fills the air,
Along with the howling of the wind in my ear.

Sophie Gallego (12)
Bishopsford Community School

My Beloved

As I linger here above the waves, waiting for night to fall
I think of my beloved, the one who makes things right.
I think of my beloved, as I fall into the night
My beloved, I need you so, the whole world needs you,
To teach us what you know.
I need you my beloved, please don't go.
My beloved, you belong here in my heart
You can see it in my eyes.
My beloved, my heart, my sun, my life, my soul,
I love you my beloved, please don't go.

Tiffany Boother (11)
Bishopsford Community School

The Sea

The sea is a big, wide blue carpet,
A different world to discover,
A blanket covering most of the world.

A big bookcase holding stories, myths and legends,
A sailor's route around the world,
A fish's home.

A deep, deep puddle of ink,
The sea is like a salt shaker carrying tons of salt,
The sea is a free place to roam where you like.

The waves are the sea's hand pushing you out and grabbing you in,
The seaweed is the sea's hair that sways from side to side in the
wind and the waves,
The sea has its dangers and safety,
The sea is a land with many mysteries.

Jamie Hargadon (12)
Bishopsford Community School

Hate Not Love

This world is full of hate not love,
Why can't peace reign above?
Everyone should have their own say,
It doesn't matter in which way.
If you're white, black, pink or blue,
You are who you are, and you are you.
Not many people like to care,
Or be nice and like to share.
So will this be the way the world ends,
Or can everyone just be friends.

Stuart Bell (13)
Bishopsford Community School

Don't Let Me Die!

There was a special school trip
In the month of May.
The kids and teachers were on a ship
On a sunny, spring day.

One of the teachers jumped in first
To find if the temperature was okay
He said the water was fine
So he set off to the bay.

Max jumped in next
But started to struggle
His mum jumped in
But started to buckle.

Max started to shout
'Am I going to die?'
His mum knew the truth
But she had to lie.

Soon she became weaker
She couldn't do much to help
Another boy jumped in
But started to yelp.

He couldn't save Max
He started to drift away
He saved Max's mum
And took her to the bay.

The teacher Paul, is in jail for a year
His parents are now, shedding their tears.

Joanne Doolan (12)
Bishopsford Community School

The Realm Of Celegurst

In the great halls of Darakadur,
Where the dwarf lord's throne lay,
Meetings were held in times of need,
And the dwarf lord rose from his throne and said one day,

'I shall tell thou a tale of old,
When dragons still roamed our lands,
When the mountains were young and mighty,
There was a dwarf realm in forgotten sands,

Located in the heart of the mountains,
Celegurst it was named,
A mighty kingdom it was,
For its structure it was famed.

The city of Celegurst was surrounded by four walls,
Greatest of these was the Southern Wall,
For it rose almost as high as the mountains,
And in the city dwelled Durdar before his fall.

Durdar was a young dwarf captain,
It was he who found the realm of Celegurst,
He dwelled in his great tower,
Until one day a storm came and the clouds burst.

Down from the sky came the Zirzargul,
An alien race that rode upon dragons,
Down they came and broke the Gate of Celegurst,
And burnt the dwarf wagons.

Wagons which brought food before winter came,
Then the Zirzargul flew to the tower,
And overthrew it,
With the fall of the tower.

The life of Durdar came to an end,
Suddenly the Zirzargul were assaulted by an unseen foe,
And they fled away from Celegurst,
But Durdar had died and the dwarfs bowed their heads low.'

Obaid Nasir (12)
Bishopsford Community School

A Watery Grave

The teacher dived in,
So Max did too.
The water so cold,
Their lips went blue.

Then caught on current,
Max was swept away,
His mother dived in,
To save the day.

He called to his mum,
'Am I going to die?'
She looked at him sad,
But did not reply.

Soon he became weaker than weak,
His arms went numb,
His body went cold,
As he fell fast asleep.

His body was nothing,
His mother let go,
For she was unconscious,
Her body afloat.

Soon they were found,
And pulled to safety,
They were taken to hospital
And remain healthy.

The teacher,
Now in jail for a year,
The boy's mum and dad,
Are shedding their tears.

Lauren O'Keefe (12)
Bishopsford Community School

The Sea

The sea is warm and shiny.
The sea is glittery blue.
The sea is wet and shimmery.
The sea reflects on you.

The sea is full of people.
The sea is full of faces.
The sea makes you feel happy.
The sea's like silky laces.

The sea is fast and wavy.
The sea is a very dark navy.
When you close your eyes in bed
You see the sea inside your head.

Lauren Henden (13)
Bishopsford Community School

The Sea

The sea is a beach bum's paradise
The sea is salty and calm on a nice day.
The sea can be as clear as the sky
The sea can be friendly and kind.
The sea is a mermaid's paradise,
The sea is a fish's home.
The sea can be rough,
The sea can be tough.
The sea is my favourite place,
I love the feeling of the sea pushing me away,
That's why I love the feeling of the sea.

Gemma Janman (12)
Bishopsford Community School

My Acrostic Poem About The Sea

A ll the fish swimming in the sea.
T he sea's like a big blue carpet.

T he sea looks like a painted picture.
H ear the noise of the sea hit the shore.
E veryone loves to play in the sea.

S hells are left on the seashore.
E verywhere you can see people swimming.
A nyone can swim in it anywhere.
S and goes between your toes.
I t's as if someone had left a tap on.
D own at the seaside are children
E verywhere you can see blue.

Samantha Little (12)
Bishopsford Community School

Punishment

P unished all the time, in my room,
U ntil I've been good,
N othing to do
I n my room, just plain boring.
S hower, eat dinner and bed is all I have to do.
H ow can I live like this?
M um, please let me out of my room. I will be good.
E ven when I'm angry, I won't have an attitude.
N ever will I treat you like that again.
T hank you Mum. I mean what I say.

Chenise Morgan (12)
Bishopsford Community School

Growing Up?

Nobody will like me when I grow up,
Nobody will offer to change my cup,
Nobody will pick up the food I drop off my spoon on the rug,
Or think of teaching me how to catch bugs.

Nobody will be there to hold my hand on the stairs,
Or get out a comb to comb my hair,
Nobody will clean my ears when they're full of dirt,
Or make me happy when I get hurt.

Nobody will sing me to sleep in the dark,
Nobody will of me a lovely jam tart,
Nobody will make me smile,
Nobody will be there to wash my clothes,
To stop them from getting into a great big pile.

Nobody will help me or stop me from eating chewing gum,
Or maybe nobody will be there to clean my bum.
Nobody will be there to let me in when I lose my keys,
But lucky for me none of these nobodies matter to me,
As I've got a lovely mummy.

Elaine Bennett (14)
Bishopsford Community School

Mum Seeing Me First Time!

You make me feel
Like when we first met,
I look at you and see me,
The same person,
I fell in love with,
And when we're together
I still want to hold your hand
To feel you're close to me,
To make me smile,
To make me see,
The love you have for me.

Hannah Francis (13)
Bishopsford Community School

Waiting To Die

My heart will soon stop
My feelings will come to an end
My life will die.

Locked up in a cell
Walls and bars
Moth-eaten mattress.

My life is a war.

Now that I am wiser I understand
When Papa would not sell the land
To the white people who had greedily planned
To buy a piece of our hearts.

So they took it out on the child
The child just happened to be me
They killed a well-known white man
Then blamed it on me.

Now I lie in a cell
In a cold, damp basement
Just waiting
Waiting to hang from a tree
The KKK will joyfully lynch me.

Kyra Mensah-Simpson (13)
Bishopsford Community School

Nature Is . . .

Nature is the luminous green grass that grows beneath the ground.
Nature is also the sun setting and filling the sky with nothing but
                                        yellow, orange and pink.
Nature is the long plants slapping against each other as the wind
                                        hits them and runs away.
Nature is the waves crashing together as the tide goes away.
Nature is beautiful.

Colleen Baptiste (12)
Bishopsford Community School

Walking Away

I want to walk away from you, but how can I leave you standing there?
After all you've done to hurt me, I still care.
I know I'm foolish for feeling this way,
But I just can't walk away. Goodbye is a hard word to say.

You don't love me and neither do I,
But leaving you would be a sad river to cry.
I know you don't care about me, but I feel for you,
And I may be a fool, but that's only for you.

You don't have to say the words - they're pointless anyway,
We both know what we have to say.
This relationship has to be ended,
But I don't know if I can face the consequences.

A life without you may mean happiness,
But the tears won't be of joy.
It may equal true love,
But you won't be by my side.

I saw the way you looked at her and your face is full of guilt,
For this I was not built.
I was not prepared for this fall,
It was your call, but I'll stand tall.

I'm walking away from you and I leave you standing there,
After all you've done to hurt me, I'm too numb to care.
I know I'm smart for feeling this way,
Because I'm walking away. Goodbye was a hard word to say.

Charlotte Winter (15)
Bishopsford Community School

Bermuda Triangle

From the east coast of Canada
Set sail a ship,
It was on its way to Jamaica,
What an exciting trip.

They were gliding through the water,
Little did they know danger lay ahead.
The ship was sailing fast,
Danger was in the path the captain had led.

Bermuda Triangle silently lay beneath the horizon,
Awaiting its next meal.
Closer and closer the ship got
As the captain turned the wheel.

Closer and closer the ship did creep,
Hungrier and hungrier did he get.
The waves got higher
And then at last they met.

Back in the island of Jamaica,
The ship did not arrive.
But little did they know,
The ship had been going through a terrible ride.

Still today ships go missing in the triangle,
And even aeroplanes.
It sounds so very crazy,
It's like David Blaine!

This is one of life's great mysteries,
But doesn't it make you think
That maybe the triangle's not magical
But did the boats just sink?

Mikaela Newton (12)
Bishopsford Community School

Poem

I remember when I went to school
As a little boy,
I stayed with the cool kids
And grew stronger every day.

When I started secondary school
I felt very old,
I understood times tables
And took my first ever exams.

When I was a teenager
I started high school,
My voice had cracked
And I grew as tall as my fridge.

When I went to college
I took my final exams,
It was harder than I thought
But I was up to the challenge.

University was the hardest,
I knew I had grown older,
I never gave up and always revised
Then got the job of my dreams.

Balal Khalid (14)
Bishopsford Community School

My Cool Mum

My mum is cool, she's good at playing pool!
My mum's cool, she works all day but always has time to play.
She does handstands and cartwheels and best of all -
She makes the best meals.
Her roasts are to die for and her puddings are yum.
Aren't I lucky to have such a good mum?
My mum loves me, she says I'm the best,
But not always because sometimes I'm a pest!
I've never known somebody as lucky as me
To have such a cool mum!

Samantha Agozzino (11)
Bishopsford Community School

Manly Man

I'm a manly man
I do everything I can.
I don't like pink
And I say what I think.
I go in the pub,
Have a few beers.
What my wife fears
I beat up old dears.
When I get in
I ask, 'Where's my dinner?'
She says, 'Why do you ask?'
I say, 'I'm getting thinner.'
She beats me with a stick
Coz she says that I'm thick.
But I tell the guys
I had a few pies
And had a fight with a man
Who's 6ft 6
And drives a blue van.
They say, 'You're 'ard,'
And then I got barred.
He said I caused trouble.
I said, 'You're 'avvin a bubble.'
Coz I'm a manly man.

Tom Rapley (14)
Bishopsford Community School

The Sea

Like a roaring lion
The waves crashing into rocks
Salty water spraying into the air
Pounding sounds as the waves break
Trickling over the pebbles on the beach
An image of hundreds of white horses galloping towards the shore
Deep and dark but calming too
The vastness of the sight ahead
The shoreline shallow, clear and clean
The sea full of aquatic life
Food supplies for many living creatures
Coral, seaweed, fish, to name just a few
It is as if somebody left a tap on.

Sean Ray (12)
Bishopsford Community School

Who Am I?

She is a convertible, leather furnished
Peugeot 206,
She is a song written about her own life,
Sad, powerful and triumphant.
She is August - rainy but sunny,
Sunny but breezy, breezy but rainy.
She is a terrible storm with the bright sunshine
Shining right behind it.
She is a red-bummed baboon
And a dark red rose.
She is a beautiful black boat
And a new, but dirty, red speed boat.
The person is Christina Aguilera.

Abbie Livesey (11)
Blenheim High School

The Dragon's Assault

Flaming eyes, flashing as it flew,
On its graceful wings it glided,
With its long tail lashing from side to side,
The wicked, wily worm passed over.

The scaly sides with jaded jewels,
Jealous jaws shooting fiery flames,
Red eyes, rich yet like a roaring flame,
Lengthy belly, pale, pallid yet proud.

The dreaded dragon circled high,
No sharp sword blade could hinder it,
No arrows, nor axe as it tore through the sky,
The River Town was left in ruins.

Jonathan Purdy (11)
Blenheim High School

The Beach

I watch the waves crash against the rocks
Like a charging bull.
The sand is as smooth as a snake's shiny skin.
The fluffy clouds float above like balloons.
The temperature is as hot as the lava from a volcano.
The trees sway on a windy day.
The sea is calm like an untouched lake.
Holidaymakers rushing around furiously
Like butterflies trapped in a jar.
Gulls flying around like golden eagles.
Fish swim in the sea as happy as my sister with sweets.
Shells buried in the sand as forgotten as a dull stone.

Parris Harknett (12)
Blenheim High School

My Monster

It needs . . .

Hands as rough as sandpaper,
Claws like a pirate's hooked hand,
Feet as big as the ocean,
His head is as big as the blazing sun,
His tongue is the colour and feels like brown bark,
His legs are as big as tree trunks,
His arms are slippery and slimy like a fish's scales,
He has a long neck like a baby giraffe,
His tail is like a school corridor,
His nose like a pig's snout.

Elizabeth Goggins (11)
Blenheim High School

My Simile Monster

His legs like tree trunks.
His tail like a never-ending story.
His belly like a raging pump.
His front arms like a bull's upper thigh.
His feet like pancake machines.
His head like a bowling ball with jaws.
His jaws like a moulding factory.
His teeth like carving knives.
His ears like mountains growing on his head.
His eyes like shiny vases.
That is my monster.

Sarah Allen (11)
Blenheim High School

What Would You Rather?

I'd rather be a dog than a cat,
I'd rather be a mouse than a rat,
I'd rather be a bird than a bat,
I'd rather have stood than sat,
I'd rather be thin than fat,
I'd rather be a sofa than a mat,
I'd rather be a bee than a gnat,
I'd rather be fit than flat,
I'd rather have a cap to a top hat.

Hayley Hyland (12)
Blenheim High School

My Dragon

Scales sharp and slimy,
Dragon breath drags dangerously,
Claws clatter courteously,
Eyes enjoy the evil,
Teeth tear through the bear,
Wings flutter as they glide through the sky,
Tail spiky and scaly,
This is my dragon,
Dangerous but dirty!

Sophie Kelly (12)
Blenheim High School

I'd Rather

I'd rather have a garden than a flower.
I'd rather live in a house than a tower.
I'd rather be sweet than sour.
I'd rather be a minute than an hour.
I'd rather be weak than have power.
I'd rather have a bath than a shower.
I'd rather it be mine than our.

Carrie-Anne Grant (11)
Blenheim High School

Sport

When athletes run
They rush.

When you kick a football
It bounces.

When a racing car goes down the circuit
It charges.

When you throw a ball
It curls.

When people swim
They splash.

James Wilkinson (11)
Blenheim High School

When The Wind Blows

When the wind blows
Leaves dance to the ground.

When the wind blows
Kites soar through the sky.

When the wind blows
Hats go flying.

When the wind blows
People start to hurry.

But when the wind goes
Everything calms down.

Rebecca Watts (12)
Blenheim High School

My Sister

My sister she has teeth like yellow grime,
She has a head like a moon covered in darkness.
My sister has a voice like a big baby crying,
She has arms like tree trunks battered.
My sister has a body like a double-decker bus,
She has a mouth like a caveman's cave.
My sister has hands like a giant's head,
She has legs like a target trucks.
My sister has hair like an octopus,
She has feet like webbed flippers.

Dean Ansell (11)
Blenheim High School

The Way We Move

When a frog wants to shop he has to hop.
When a cat wants a mouse it must pounce.
When a whale is tired it floats.
When a child is home from school she plays in the pool.
When an ant sees a foot, it goes running.
When a fish sees a whale it swims the other way.
When a cat spies milk she licks her lips for drinking.
When my hamster smells me he runs to the cage door in glee.
When it is time for bed I slouch up the stairs to sleep.

Hannah Alsop (11)
Blenheim High School

The Hurricane

It broke through the door gusting up a storm,
Rampaging down the corridor like a bull in a china shop,
Swooping up all the desks, destroying everything in its path,
And after a while it started to die down
But even though everything was destroyed it was all back to normal.

Lee Smith (11)
Blenheim High School

The Ocean

The calm beautiful ocean is as gentle as can be,
Or is it?

The violent ocean drowns and kills,
Sets its creatures to eat us alive,
And even sinks boats with ice.
The mean ocean is scary and violent,
Or is it?

The playful ocean lets us swim,
Gives us a warm safe feeling,
And even fills us with joy.
The playful ocean is safe and joyful
Or is it?

The roaring ocean is angry with us,
Protective as can be,
And even will crash onto us.
The roaring ocean is angry and protective,
Or is it?

No,
The ocean is almost anything,
But may surprise you and me.

George Wales (11)
Blenheim High School

The Twister

It crashed through the corridor,
The papers were like aeroplanes flying round the classrooms.
It whizzed round the hall searching for something to destroy,
Chairs were on the ceiling and lights were on the floor,
It was like a screaming child, always getting what it wants.

Faye Phillips (11)
Blenheim High School

How To Make A Monster

It needs . . .

Teeth like a baseball bat,
A head like an elephant,
A mouth like a football,
A body like a big bottle,
Legs like spaghetti,
Arms like a train,
Ears like sails,
Eyes like pirates,
Claws like hangers,
Nose like wood.

Anthony Bines (11)
Blenheim High School

Haiku

Roars like a wild beast,
But glistens like a diamond,
Is it ever calm?

Free for the public,
As we watch it waste its time,
Always the same place.

The beaches are full,
It is a sight for your eyes,
It's magnificent.

Kristina Twigge-Molecey (11)
Blenheim High School

Storm Haiku

Powerful winds blow,
The storm throws us miles off course,
Waves crash on our ship.

David Hurst (11)
Blenheim High School

My Dragon

My dragon has terrible teeth that tear,
He has envious eyes,
His scaly skin is silky smooth,
His tail is as long as a tower,
His wing will whoosh him up,
His breath as fiery as a ferocious phoenix.

Rhianna Edwards (11)
Blenheim High School

What Would You Rather?

I'd rather have coffee than tea,
I'd rather be a bee than a flea,
I'd rather have glee than a key,
I'd rather be the sea than a tree,
I'd rather say yes than wee,
I'd rather be a she than a he.

Lorna Joyce (11)
Blenheim High School

Think!

When a thought comes in your head,
Close your mouth and *think* instead.
Then you won't get into *trouble*
Because you've used your thinking *bubble*.
So, 'Sorry Miss,' you say instead,
Then you won't get sent to the head!

Ryan Lockyer (11)
Blenheim High School

What Would You Rather?

I'd rather have coffee than tea
Because tea isn't right for me.
I'd rather be me than you
Because I heard you had the flu.
I'd rather be a tree than a flower
Because trees can grow as tall as a tower.
I'd rather be a key than a door
Because doors always touch the floor.
I'd rather be happy than sad
Because being sad feels really bad.
I'd rather be two than three
Because three isn't right for me.
I'd rather be strong than weak
Because strong gets me through the week.

Matthew Grant (11)
Blenheim High School

On The Move!

When elephants trip they skip.
When hawks are told to walk they stalk.
When rabbits snuffle they shuffle.
When rats see cats they sit.
When camels spit they sit.
When mice are small they crawl.
When dogs slobber they hover.
When starfish wish they swish.
When snakes jiggle they wiggle.
When lions pretend to sleep they creep.
When camels are in a hump they jump.

Charlotte Taroghion (11)
Blenheim High School

My Monster's Pet Rhino

My monster's pet rhino is as fierce as can be,
He would have you or me for his tea.
His head is like a school
And his body, the size of Mount Rushmore,
Ears like rotating fans.

My monster's pet rhino is as strong as can be,
He could even kill me.
His mouth is as small as a grain of sand,
His teeth are the size of a computer system
And eyes like oranges.

My monster's pet rhino
Is as fierce, as strong
And as smart as can be,
He must be my monster's pet rhino.

Matthew Downey (11)
Blenheim High School

A Summer's Day

The sun was shining oh so bright,
My face was tingling in the light,
The trees were swaying ever so slight,
With flowers blooming, catching the sight,
We smell the air so fresh and warm,
We lay together upon the lawn,
With drinks in hand and food galore,
The birds will sing and fly away,
To find a place not so warm,
The sun will dip beneath the clouds,
Night will fall, not even a sound.

Amy Savage (11)
Blenheim High School

My Dragon

My dragon has tearing teeth to tear you
Up into little pieces.
He has razor-sharp claws as sharp as a dagger.
He has skin as rough as sandpaper.
He has wings to fly as high as the sky.
He breathes fire as hot as a furnace.
He has big staring eyes as devious
And dastardly as the Devil.
He is not hungry today because his belly is
Full of naughty knights and wizards!

Rebecca Loosley (11)
Blenheim High School

Monster Of The Loch

They say it lives in the deep of the lake,
It strikes when it likes
And makes the villagers quake.

It swims stealthily through the loch,
Darting eyes, a constant surprise,
Its scaly body sweeps past the rock.

It lurks in the shadows, so fishermen beware,
They fear what they hear,
Avoid the monster's lair.

Kearney Cook-Abbott (12)
Blenheim High School

Heatwave Haiku

The fiery hot sun,
Hotter than a man has known,
No one could survive.

Richard Shepherd (11)
Blenheim High School

Dragon Poem

His eyes are bold as mould,
His palms are sweaty, killing people already.
Ready to shine his spikes, so sweaty,
Wings flapping steady
In the air like a scarecrow flying,
As fast as a Mercedes-Benz.
His nose is big and slimy like a slug,
Smoke coming out so black and dense,
Teeth sharp as a knife ready to cut flesh,
So strong, so wrong.

Sam Rhodes (11)
Blenheim High School

Buffalo

I like animals with big horns
That just lie lazily on the lawns.
It trots off into the sun
Then it begins to run.
The lion sprints and bites its throat
Then it looks at its little goat.
Now the buffalo begins to die
And its little 'un begins to cry.
As the tears fall from its cheeks
The birds fly down and peck with beaks.

Sam Kilpatrick (11)
Blenheim High School

Science Is Fun

Lightning flashes,
Then comes the sound,
It's thunder
I'll be bound,
Light is faster than the sound.

Jake Phillp (11)
Blenheim High School

My Big Sister

I don't like my big sister . . .

She's got eyes like a cheetah when it's on the lookout for prey,
She's got hair like a monkey when it has just been dried in a dry
cleaners and not brushed,
She's got skin like the colour of a pale moon in May,
She's got a voice like a hyena in the wild,
She's got ears like an elephant's ears, but twice the size,
She's got a nose like a little pig,
She's got feet like a giant's feet,
She's got arms and legs like a snake's body,
She's got hands like rotten jelly,
She's got lips like a great white shark.

Still, even though I don't like her, it doesn't mean I don't love her.

Hannah Vincent (11)
Blenheim High School

Untouchable

His feet are as tough as nails.
His legs are curled and waiting to let go.
His shoulders hard with power.
His hair is soft and flowing.
His head held proud, so beautiful.
The sun catches his eye, so enchanting, so bright,
A window to his soul.
Untouchable; a fiery spirit about to run free.
You can take him to water but can't make him drink.
As old as time, his legacy
Horse!

Lucy Pidgeon (11)
Blenheim High School

Alliteration Poem

One whistling warthog walking wildly to Wimbledon.
Two troublesome twins tickled each other to death.
Three thatched horses thumped thoroughly through the night.
Four fearsome fluorescent fireflies flew through the fire.
Five frantic firemen fiercely fought through the fire.
Six special superstars span straight down Seccil Street.
Seven Spanish snakes slithered sneakily into the local park.
Eight annoying elephants eagerly ignored America.
Nine nutters gnawing at a foot.
Ten ferocious tarantulas tickling horrendously next door's cats.

Jack Wood (11)
Blenheim High School

My Monster Looks Like This . . .

His mouth's like rain,
    His teeth are like blades,
        His head's like a balloon
            And his belly is like a train.
                He smells like a horse,
He hears like an elephant,
    His nose is like sick worms having a race
        And his voice, well I'm not going to go into that!

Jessica Ramsey (11)
Blenheim High School

Sound Of The Sea

The sea swishes over the sand, sliding slowly,
It crashes against the rocks like a hammer hitting a nail,
Lashing out at the beaches, it slowly washes away miserably.

Stephen Pryce (11)
Blenheim High School

My Monster

His voice was like the deep blue ocean.
His feet were like huge cars.
His teeth were like the sharp crushers at the dump.
His arms were like big telephone poles.
His mouth was like the whites of the sea.
His fur was like soft cotton wool.
His brain was like small grains of sugar.
His skin was like old boots.
His fingers were like a spaghetti junction, all curly and twisty
And he is my monster.

Jordan Fitzpatrick (11)
Blenheim High School

My Sister

Her lips are like red blood, bright and colourful.
Her hair is like a bundle of gold silk.
Her body is as small and skinny as a mouse.
Her voice is very firm for when she demands.
Her ears are as small as a baby's, hidden by her gold silk hair.
Her hands are as small as a mouse's head.
Her feet are small - smaller than mine.
That's my sister.

Naomi Waters (12)
Blenheim High School

Winter Wonders . . .

Winter is as cold as a murderer's heart.
Winter feels like icy hands sweeping over you.
Winter looks like a box lined with sheets of white paper.
Winter sounds like millions of marbles dropping onto the stone floor.
Winter smells like nothing when your nose is blocked!

Deena Ahmed (11)
Blenheim High School

Alliteration Poem

One whistling warthog walking wildly to Wimbledon.
Two troublesome twins tickled each other to death.
Three thatched houses thumped thoroughly through the night.
Four fierce fireflies went fluorescent when they flew through the fire.
Five frogs frighten the frightening flamingos.
Six snakes slowly salsa danced through sexy streets.
Seven snails slithered slowly, shaking their shells.
Eight Easter eggs ate eggs everywhere.
Nine knights nicked each other's knickers.
Ten teachers tried to teach twelve times tables to their tired teenage
pupils.

Adam Keehn (11)
Blenheim High School

Alliteration

One whistling warthog walking wildly to Wimbledon.
Two troublesome twins tickled each other to death.
Three thatched houses thumped thoroughly through the night.
Four fearsome fluorescent fireflies flew through the fire.
Five fierce firefighters flew fast through the sky.
Six smelly slugs sliding sideways.
Seven slippery snails sipping some soup.
Eight enormous elephants eating enormous eggs.
Nine nasty neighbours nailing Nan's fence.
Ten terrible teachers telling Tim not to talk.

Natasha Bayley (11)
Blenheim High School

How To Make A Monster

It needs . . .

A head like an egg,
A nose like a cherry,
Eyes like chocolate eclairs,
A mouth like a slice of pepper,
A body like a chocolate muffin,
Legs like breadsticks,
Arms like pepperoni,
Hair like cheese string,
Teeth like sugar cubes,
Feet like bananas,
Hands like chocolate fingers.

Tiffany Wayman (11)
Blenheim High School

My Monster

My monster has . . .

An eye like a large sphere,
Teeth like sharp daggers,
Stench like rotten onions,
Height like a giraffe,
A head like a giant scab,
Muscles like large boulders,
An eyebrow like a spiky hedgehog,
Nails like short swords,
Hair like thick ropes,
A nose like a thunderstruck tree,
An appetite for me!

Max Robinson (11)
Blenheim High School

In The Beginning

When I was one I sucked my thumb,
When I was two I got a new shoe,
When I was three I got stung by a bee,
When I was four I got a new door,
When I was five I learnt how to jive,
When I was six I got the nits,
When I was seven my grandpa was in Heaven,
When I was eight I was as tall as the gate,
When I was nine I got out of line,
When I was ten I got a rabbit called Ken,
Now I am eleven I really like melon.

Naomi Snelling (11)
Blenheim High School

My Brother Chris

Chris is a creaky floorboard
He's naughtier than 'page three'
He's the Grinch out to ruin Christmas
He's weirder than hearing a cat bark
He's the messiest pig on the farm
He's a pair of football boots
Chris is my brother
And he's the sloppiest teenager I know!

Becky Hindle (12)
Blenheim High School

How To Make A Horse

Ears as pointy as triangles,
Legs as thin as twigs,
Tail as fluffy as a poodle,
Eyes as calm as the sea,
Fur as smooth as silk,
Body as strong as a tree trunk.

Kim Bartram (11)
Blenheim High School

On The Move

When lions gobble
They like to wobble,
When cubs are eating
Their mother is sleeping,
When donkeys stumble
They mumble,
When birds fly
They are very shy,
When toddlers shout
They run about,
When dolphins swim
They waggle their fin,
When dogs bark
They like to lark,
When frogs get stroked
They like to croak,
When squirrels nibble
They like to dribble,
When ladybirds fly
It looks like a spy.

Alice Hoy (11)
Blenheim High School

Eminem

He is a freezing, bone chilling day in winter,
He is a terrifying and dangerous thunderstorm,
He is a ferocious, killing man-eating lion,
He is a luxurious, soft-top sports car,
He is a rough, wooden unsanded chair,
He is a fast, beat piece of music.

Sean Harris (11)
Blenheim High School

Heaven Or Seven?

Where am I? Where could I be?
Puffy clouds and clear blue skies surround me.
I'm searching through the clouds for what could be revealed.
I find an entrance, unlike the others it hasn't been sealed.
Should I walk through? Should I go on the other side?
Or maybe I should go back? I'll get home, there'll be a ride.
If I go back, I'll be led to my world.
But what if when I return, my life has been sold?
Should I go forward? Should I go back?
Either way, I wouldn't need to leave a track.
My curiosity did not get the better of me.
So here I am today, gazing at the sea.
I now truly understand that I would've been free.
I have nothing left, my only companion is my tree.
Was I dreaming? Could I have really gone to Heaven?
But one thing's for sure, I didn't wake up at seven.

Nazia Sooruth (13)
Blenheim High School

My Little Sister

I've got a little sister
They say she's my skin and blister
She has ginger hair
And skin so fair

She is my little sister

She likes to watch Balamory
Whilst listening to her favourite story
We splash in the bath together
I wish she'd stay little forever

She is my little sister.

Harry McKeown (11)
Blenheim High School

The Sea

Waves going *crash, crash* like an aeroplane
The white froth washed up on the shore like the top of a pint of beer
Rocks as sharp as knives
The hush in the air as all you hear is the sea lashing against the shore
There is almost an earthquake as each wave gives a separate,
                                                    special shake
The seagulls' wings give a swish and a swirl on each flap
The surfboards slide along the water like skaters on ice.

Sam Swindells (11)
Blenheim High School

My Mum

My mum is always happy-looking
as if she is at a wedding.
My mum is so tidy, making sure the house
looks brand new and furnished.
My mum's mind works like a computer.
My mum is so funny
that she could be a millionaire comedian.

Sarah Lyon (11)
Blenheim High School

Miss Howard

She is as bold as a buffalo
Her voice is as croaky as a frog
She has eyes like an eagle in the night
Her shoes are like a penguin's waddling along
She has a card round her neck like a necklace
Her smile is like a monkey - so cheeky.

Steve Baker (11)
Blenheim High School

My Brother

His head is like a balloon that's pink,
His ears stick out like an elf's!
His feet are so big they couldn't fit in a sink
And his eyes are as large as bowls!

His nose is like a plum tomato,
His arms are as bony as twigs!
His teeth are as yellow as custard,
His mouth is as wide as a bridge!

Courtney Barella (11)
Blenheim High School

Weird Waves

Tidal waves crashing against the rocks,
Storming and thundering, will it ever stop?
Suddenly silence, which is extremely weird,
No more waves crashing against the rocks.
Not a cloud in the royal-blue sky,
Not even a sound could be heard for miles.
How can this be? It was ever so noisy.

Daniel Wright (11)
Blenheim High School

The Sea

The sea is like water left in a bath tub.
The sea is like water coming out of a tap.
The sea is like flowers being blown in the wind.
The sea is like ice floating in a glass of water.
The sea is like throwing rubbish in the bin.
The sea is like pencil to paper.
The sea is like the end of a story.

Francesca Nott (11)
Blenheim High School

When . . .

When kangaroos hop,
they stop.
When rabbits move,
the babies groove.
When hamsters squeak,
the gerbils peek.
When cheetahs run,
they have fun.
When horses trot,
they sleep a lot.
When crocodiles snap,
their teeth crack.
When tigers grumble,
they normally stumble.

Hannah Conibeer (11)
Blenheim High School

My Clever Grandad

My grandad is a fussy king
sitting on his throne all day.
My grandad is a funny penguin
trying to run on ice.
My grandad is a clever calculator
being used in an exam.
My grandad is a tidy bedroom
with all the sheets washed.
My grandad is a playful bouncy castle
letting the kids bounce on him.
My grandad is an angry bull
charging towards the red flag.

Ben Hodgkins (11)
Blenheim High School

The Snowy Man

A snowy man,
Loves a fan,
He hates a fire,
He's not a liar.

Standing in
The snowy white scene,
Likes a play
Because he's so keen.

An icy body,
A bright red hat,
A carrot nose,
Nice and fat.

Standing in the garden,
On cotton wool,
It's not so bad,
Because he loves the cool!

Amy Housego (11)
Blenheim High School

Don't Wake Up

Mist so cloudy like a dream
Walking on rainbows really
A stream
Floating clouds like
Floating flowers
What seem like minutes are
Really hours
But this dream is soon to be
A long forgotten memory.

Alex Hale (11)
Blenheim High School

How To Make A Monster

It needs . . .

A head like a pineapple
A body like an apple
Ears like two bananas
Eyes like two strawberries
A mouth like half a melon
Teeth like a shark
Legs and arms like loads of oranges
Claws like grapes
A tail like two big watermelons.

Maddie Cooper (11)
Blenheim High School

How To Make A Monster

It needs . . .

A head like an Oxford dictionary,
A body like a school desk,
A nose like a white board,
Eyes like open exercise books,
A mouth like a chest of drawers,
Teeth like board pens,
Ears like blazers,
Whiskers like pencils all blunt,
Legs and arms like straight rulers, all stiff,
A tongue like a long tie.

Harry Rodd (11)
Blenheim High School

How To Make A Monster

It needs . . .

A head like a football stadium
A body like a basketball
Hair like spaghetti
Arms like cricket bats
Legs like tree trunks
A mouth like a football net
Ears like white boards
Fingers like twigs
A tail like a snake
And eyes like melons.

Aaron Johnson (12)
Blenheim High School

How To Make A Monster

It needs . . .

A head like a big jaw-breaker
A mouth like a cut bit of pizza
Eyes like two dustbin lids
Ears like two pillows
A body like a ruler
Fingers like fish fingers
Claws like iron nails
Wings like two big leaves
A tongue like an elastic band.

Callum Wilkinson (11)
Blenheim High School

Alliteration

One whistling warthog walked wildly to Wimbledon.
Two troublesome twins tickled each other to death.
Three thatched houses thumped thoroughly through the night.
Four fearsome fluorescent fireflies flew through the fire.
Five freaky friends fought until the death.
Six stupid singers sang a stupid song.
Seven silly scientists smelt of chemicals.
Eight elephants were eating eagles' eggs.
Nine knobbly knees lined up against the trees.
Ten tigers tore some tomatoes into pieces.

Oliver Gaynor (11)
Blenheim High School

One To Ten

One whistling warthog walked wildly to Wimbledon.
Two troublesome twins tickled each other to death.
Three thatched houses thumped thoroughly through the night.
Four fearsome frogs fought for their food.
Five frightening fish flicked Fred's feet.
Six slithering snakes slithered south.
Seven sizzling sausages steamed in a pan.
Eight African elephants used Indian oranges.
Nine nuisance nits nicked Neil's hair.
Ten tragic turtles took the crown jewels.

Tristan White (11)
Blenheim High School

Tiger, Tiger

Tiger, tiger orange and black
Down on the ground I can see your tracks.
So! Tiger, tiger orange and black
I'm going home so you don't jump on my back!

Harriett Church Jennings (11)
Blenheim High School

Alliteration

One whistling warthog walking to Wimbledon.
Two troublesome twins tickled each other to death.
Three thatched houses thumped through the night.
Four fearsome fireflies flying through the fire.
Five floppy frogs flopping everywhere.
Six hissing snakes sneaking slowly.
Seven scary sharks swimming slowly in the sea.
Eight elephants eating extremely annoyingly.
Nine naughty nits nibbling naughtily on people's hair.
Ten torturing tigers terrorising town.

George Parnell (12)
Blenheim High School

Lightning In School

It smashed through the window like a hail of hurricanes
It banged against the door
It lifted tables and chairs 50-feet high and threw them
It entered the canteen yelling and screaming
It cracked the stage before it left the hall and went sizzling out
the window
Shooting at the sky twisting and turning before entering the
next school.

Joshua Beecher (11)
Blenheim High School

Delightful Dad

My dad is a cat spending ages toasting by the fire.
My dad is a herd of penguins at feeding time at the zoo.
My dad is my grandma's eyes.
My dad is a walking Oxford dictionary.
My dad is a newborn baby learning how to walk.
My dad is a soft fur rug next to the fire in winter.

Sophie Owen (11)
Blenheim High School

My Dad

My dad has eyes like the moon
His arms are like a big swing
Hair like a black wave
He has teeth like soldiers
His hands are like two saucepans
His mouth is like a banana
He has a voice like a bear
And toes like rulers
He has a chin like a bun
And a head like a boiled egg.

Ashleigh Bruen (11)
Blenheim High School

My Friendly Monster

He has a head like a carrot
A body like a fat pizza
Arms that look like chimneys
Ears that are like bananas
A mouth like an apple
Legs that look like scaffolding poles
Eyes that look like dinner plates
Fingers like fat sausages
Toes that look like melons
A tail like a slimy snake.

Hannah Kraushaar (11)
Blenheim High School

Under The Sea

Fishes swimming everywhere,
Colours flashing by,
Seaweed brushing past your face,
What a beautiful world.

Lucy Smith (11)
Blenheim High School

Crash Bang Wallop!

I walk down the stairs, they creak!
I eat my breakfast, the cereal crackles!
My mum writes a note to school about my lateness,
She tears the page in half - *rip!*
I fell over, my knee cut!
I walked into a lamp post, *crash!*
I got hit in the arm with a rock!
I saw a boy on a tree having a climb!
In music lesson the cymbals went *clang!*
I had lunch -
The dinner ladies served my lunch from a tin, *scrape!*
I ate my crisps, *crunch!*

Samantha Henry (11)
Blenheim High School

Haiku

The golden leaves fall
Crunching while he jumps on them
While his bag wobbles.

Elliot Draper (11)
Blenheim High School

Skiing

Two years ago we did go,
For a holiday in the snow.
The snow all crunchy under our feet,
The trail that we left behind was ever so neat.
Off to the mountains we hiked,
Which we all liked.
Up on high touching the sky,
Watching snowflakes drift by.

Christie Grimwood (11)
Blenheim High School

Number Poem

One whistling warthog walking wildly to Wimbledon.
Two troublesome twins tickled each other to death.
Three thatched houses thumped through the night.
Four fearsome fluorescent fireflies flew through the fire.
Six sad sandbags slid down Splash Street.
Seven scary skulls slid slowly down Slowly Hill.
Eight elephants exercised.
Nine naked nappies napped.

Ryan Jordan (11)
Blenheim High School

Sounds Of The Sea

As I sit on the rock and listen real hard,
The sounds that I hear come from near and far.
The crash of the waves rip against the sea,
They cut like a knife, but don't come near me.
With a crunch and a crash, a crackle and a clang,
I hear the sea scrape with a bang.
As the sea calms down you can hear a creak
And all the sea life goes to sleep.

Dean Sale (11)
Blenheim High School

The Ways Of The Sea

The sound of the waves can hush you to sleep,
But when it touches you itself, you awake with a shake,
As its sharp coldness hits you like a knife.

Crash, crash, crash goes the sea with a lash against the cliff wall
And with a swish it crashes onto the sand.
It will start to swirl and make a whirlpool.
The water slides over the rocks and appears to give them a wash.

Sean Starkey (12)
Blenheim High School

Thunderstorm

It smashed through the ceiling and splintered the stage.
It sped down the steps and into the hall.
A butler stood waiting, firm and tall.
It passed through his body with a crash like the sea.
Then with a soft thud he fell dead to the floor.
It shattered the front door released to the night,
Illuminating almost anything in sight.

Geoffrey Sparham (11)
Blenheim High School

When . . .

When dancers dance, they prance,
When people run about, they shout.
When cats are on the prowl, they growl,
When fishes flow, they're slow.
When dolphins thrive, they dive.

Kirstie Locke (11)
Blenheim High School

If I Was A Pirate . . .

If I was a pirate
I would own a parrot
The parrot would own a carrot
The carrot's name would be Barrett

Barrett would kill the parrot
The pirate would be sad
He would shout at the carrot
And say he was bad

The pirate would leave home
The carrot would be lonely
It would be a happy ending -
If only!

Amberley Self (12)
Esher CE High School

Love To Hate

I know, I know I've let you down
I've been a fool to myself
I thought that I could live for no one else
But now through all the hurt and pain
It's time for me to respect
The ones you love mean more than anything

So, with sadness in my heart
Feel the best thing that I could do
Is end it all and leave forever
What's done is done, it feels so bad
What once was happy now is sad
I'll never love again
My world is ending

I wish that I could turn back time
Cos now the guilt is all mine
Can't live without
The trust from those you love
I know we can't forget the past
You can't forget love and pride
Because of that, it's killing me inside

It all returns to nothing
It all comes tumbling down, tumbling down, tumbling down
It all returns to nothing
I just keep letting me down, letting me down, letting me down

In my heart of hearts
I know that I could never love again
I've lost everything, everything
Everything that matters to me
Matters in this world

I wish that I could turn back time
Cos now the guilt is all mine
Can't live without the trust from those you love
I know we can't forget the past
You can't forget love and pride
Because of that, it's killing me inside

It all returns to nothing
It just keeps tumbling down, tumbling down, tumbling down
It all returns to nothing
I just keep letting me down, letting me down, letting me down
It all returns to nothing
It just keeps tumbling down, tumbling down, tumbling down
It all returns to nothing
I just keep letting me down, letting me down, letting me down.

Louis Whittle (14)
Esher CE High School

Do You Ever Sometimes . . . ?

Do you ever sometimes feel like you wanna give up the fight?
Do you ever sometimes think that you can't tell day from night?
Do you ever sometimes believe that you are all alone?
Do you ever sometimes dream that you don't have a home?

Do you ever sometimes wonder why things don't go your way?
Do you ever sometimes think why life's black and white, not grey?
Do you ever sometimes ask why you're not me and I'm not you?
Do you ever sometimes ask questions, when you don't know what
                                                            to do?

Do you ever sometimes feel like you want to kick and scream?
Do you ever sometimes think about where you're going or where
                                                you've been?
Do you ever sometimes wish that life would disappear?
Do you ever sometimes think of the enemy or your fear?

Do you ever sometimes wonder why people write their feelings down?
Do you ever sometimes think about twisting a smile into a frown?
Do you ever sometimes just want to live your life again once more?
Do you ever sometimes think that there's a new start behind that door?

Katie Ovington (15)
Esher CE High School

In The Hope Of Tomorrow . . .

In the hope of tomorrow,
I'll close my eyes.
To see you in the morning,
No more goodbyes.

In the hope of tomorrow,
I'll tuck you in.
Love me tonight
And forgive my sin.

In the hope of tomorrow,
I'll let you sleep.
I'll be here tomorrow,
It's you I'm gonna keep.

In the hope of tomorrow,
I'll stay with you.
Share this night with me
And the morning too.

In the hope of tomorrow,
I'll make love with you tonight.
I wanna be like this always,
This feels so right.

In the hope of tomorrow,
I'll give you a kiss,
'Cause if tomorrow doesn't come,
Then it's you I'll miss.

And in the hope of tomorrow,
I'll love you forever, today.

Ella Smith (15)
Esher CE High School

The Man And The Moon

The moon is settled in the sky
Always gleaming bright and high
The stars circle overhead
Whilst the man in the moon sleeps in his bed.

His snores awake the Milky Way
While comfy in his bed he lay
But down below the world is light
But his day is actually night!

The moon glides around the black night sky
Then something catches the man's beady eye
It is a planet which glows a fiery blood-red
But he doesn't know its name so he thinks in his head.

He wonders out loud which planet it could be,
He said, 'If only it was a bit closer, then I would see.'
He thought and he thought which planet was red
And then it came to him and he jumped out of bed.

'It's Mars!' he said, shouting out loud
And this was the first moment he had ever felt so proud
'The planet just slipped out of my mind,' he said with glee
And now he has remembered, he is again happy.

Hannah Slatter (12)
Esher CE High School

The End Of The Earth

The end of the Earth
Will begin with the surf,
Which will get smaller with every day.
Then the light will go out
And people will shout
For *help* is the last thing they'll say.
Then the world will go *boom*
And we will face doom
As that is the fate of the Earth.

Greg Whitby (11)
Kingston Grammar School

Dragons

Scales glistening like crystals,
Talons as long as cars,
Eyes lit up with fire,
Teeth the size of a bus,
Roaring, snarling, burning, raging fury.

Mouth the size of a house,
Spikes and spines on the tail,
Body bright blood-red,
Fire as hot as a fiery furnace,
Roaring, snarling, burning, raging fury.

Feet the size of Big Ben,
Tail as long as a fifteen-carriage train,
Wings like flattened hot air balloons,
Snout alive with fire,
Roaring, snarling, burning, raging fury,
Hell is not a land, it's in a dragon.

Oliver Woodings (11)
Kingston Grammar School

Remains

Pacing through the ruins of a shattered world
A boneless hand with fingers curled
Stalking this land 'til eternity ends
When all is destroyed, what's left but pretend?

If the land comes to darkness, without soul or life
Then Death will come knocking, with Terror his knife
When beauty has fallen, when nothing is clean
When love is abandoned, what's left but to dream?

When hope turns to fear, when the sky turns to black,
When breathing is dying, when the clocks won't turn back
When mountains have crumbled and rivers run dry,
When now is forever, what's left but to lie?

Ben Kumar (14)
Kingston Grammar School

The River

The river begins up high
   It starts from a spring
      Just a trickle to begin with,
         Fast-running water it brings
            Cutting its path through the rocks,
         Now it's more of a stream.
      Crashing down the waterfall
         River is widening, it seems,
            Slowly meandering its course,
               Across the flat land,
                  The river is broadening now.
            It is really quite grand,
         It is reaching the end of its course,
            The river has reached full size,
         It empties itself into the sea
   And waves the land goodbye.

Michael Stenning (12)
Kingston Grammar School

Mirrors

Forever watching, always there,
They cannot move, can only glare.
Casting looks across the room,
Many hours they can consume.

You look at them, they look at you
But is there more that they can do?
Cast their eyes into the past,
Remember who they looked at last?

Or are they depthless, in 2D
Cannot be opened with a key?
Just sitting pretty on the wall,
Or plain or fat or large or small?

Katie O'Neill (14)
Kingston Grammar School

Elephant

It plods through the jungle,
Slow yet elegantly,
Munching on leaves
Aware of the prowling lions.

Approaching the waterhole,
The elephant is like royalty,
Big and proud.
The other animals make room,
For this magnificent creature.

Yet the elephant is always running,
He may not look it but he is,
Running from the poachers
Running from man.

Man cuts down his home,
Man kills his family,
He is alone,
Alone in this hot savannah.

They want his tusks,
The shining white ivory,
Used for nothing except show,
Man can be cruel.

Sarika Rice (12)
Kingston Grammar School

Mother Nature

Conflicting emotions
Anger and savagery drive the forces
To send soft toadstools through six feet of concrete
To demolish entire villages in the blink of an eye
Love and care then drive the forces
In control of creation and repair
This is how unstable nature really is;
Balanced on a knife edge
That may just be snapped by us.

Alex Grounds (13)
Kingston Grammar School

David Blaine

There he sits
In his glass box,
Looming over the crowd.
He is waiting -
Waiting until 44 days
Have passed.
Why?
People ask.
Why at all?
Is he mad
Or is this an illusion
Of the human eye?
Sipping water
Day in
Day out
Hunger and
Boredom are striking.
Will he last
This 44 day barrier -
Or will he fall?
Magic.

Kabir Sandhu (12)
Kingston Grammar School

A Horse

Galloping in the rain, sun and wind,
His hooves thundering through the Earth,
Not a care in his mind,
As the sun streams through the field.

His soft brown coat, shimmering in the light,
Running through the plains till sunset.
Not a care in his mind
And in peace, waiting for the start of a new day.

Aimée Connolly (12)
Kingston Grammar School

My Street

As I walk down the street,
I hear the patter of my feet.

I can hear and see so many things.

People walking,
People talking.

People driving,
People skiving.

People cycling,
People hiking.

People shopping,
People hopping.

People using buses
People making big fusses.

People going to school,
People trying to look cool.

Traffic zooming down the road,
I try to remember the Highway Code.

I can hear the train, whooshing past
It sounds as if it's going fast.

As I walk down my street, I hear the patter of my feet.

Geraldine Evans (13)
Kingston Grammar School

Through The Year

The new shoots of spring burst through
The lifeless ground bringing the green
Joy of the season, new life
Brought by a pale sun and sustained
By a gentle rain.

Summer in all its crimson glory
Bursts through the clouds, a robust
Sun dispersing the clouds and charring the Earth.
Seaward tempests crash against the shore
As tourists bask on the golden sand.

The world ages as autumn encroaches,
Filled with fog and mist.
Piles of leaves stir under a warm breeze
Painting the streets in gold.

The sharp gales of winter
Slice through the forests and as
The snow swirls in storms of white
We are warm and safe in the comfort of
Dawning spring.

Laurence Todd (14)
Kingston Grammar School

Abuse

Over in the corner is Sarah
Just standing there staring at the wall
With bruises all over her body
And tears running down her cheeks
She's trying to hide her hurt
From her dad, for if he saw the tears he
Would shout bad words
And call her names, that would make him
Even more insane.

Susanna Goffe (12)
Kingston Grammar School

Summer's Rain

I wake up to find
The beating of the summer's rain,
My eyes, creak open
And I get out of bed.
I stand in front of the window
And watch the sprinkle
Slowly come down from the hurried sky.

The rain comes down faster and harder,
It gets louder just as the thunder cracks
And the lightning is thrown from the sky.
I jump as the door flings open
And slams into the wall.

I quickly turn around
With a stretched and frightened face,
I see him standing there,
He could see that I was scared
And he rushes out to hold me.
Wraps me in his arms
And comforts me and whispers, 'It's all right.'

Just like that, the storm ends,
The rain gathers together and
The clouds run away.
The flowers sparkle and shine
In the warm sun.
Just after the summer's rain
I thank him for coming to save me
And I ask him to stay a bit longer.
He smiles at me and then he slowly fades away.

Andrew Chan (14)
Kingston Grammar School

The Motorway At Night

The motorway,
a long, winding tongue
projects from the mouth of the city.
Black as soot,
it meanders its way through the luscious countryside.
Now the tongue of a snake,
it forks at a junction
only to meet again after the twists and turns
resembling a three-dimensional maze.

The lamps,
standing tall, like giants,
that peer down onto the red and white blurs,
hold a glowing planet in each hand.
They raise the contours of the terrain
to form a perpetual roller coaster
suspended from sleeping clouds.

The catseyes,
crystal clear gems,
sparkling like stars, they guide passing drivers.
All the different colours: red, blue, green and white
create a runway that continues on into the distance
and over the horizon,
like a never-ending rainbow road.

At last it comes to an end.
Returning home,
the illuminations become clearer.
The grey carpet is laid out
ready for the drivers to disappear into the city
of bright lights.

Calum Smith (14)
Kingston Grammar School

The Morning

The continued burring of the alarm
Echoes through my half closed ears
As painful as drilling through my skull.
The silence on the streets
And the looming daylight outside my window
Seems to hover in the mist.

From the tender warmth where I sleep,
I am forced to strip myself from my blankets
And I shiver from the cold.
Still half asleep, I dress myself,
But into strict, unchangeable uniform
Where I spend my years.

I can taste the bitterness of the frosty air
As it hovers and lurks around the town.
I try and fight the wind as it whips my face
Like a mistress with a disobedient schoolboy.
I feel, as I walk from my home,
Morning has been left behind,
And I wait for tomorrow where
I am tortured again.

Lottie Naughton-Rumbo (14)
Kingston Grammar School

The Morning

The morning dew lay scattered
over the blades of grass
Shimmering in the early sun.
The mighty wind flies through
the leaves of the trees
leaving faces in the sky.
The chilling frost, freezing my fingers
swirls around my frozen body,
the hovering mist balancing
on the morning air,
stands still, not knowing where to go.

Nicola Gale (13)
Kingston Grammar School

Unfinished Painting

Slowly an outline appears,
Emerging from the canvas, coming to life
It's left hanging, abandoned on the wall.

I can see it clearly now, as I move away,
Reaching out, those eyes following every move I make,
Shadows move behind
Nothing, just darkness.
Those eyes just candles in the distance,
Still I feel them.
Fearing my body, searching for clues.
It's all cold, no moon shines through.

I feel something touch me,
Just a cold breeze and a door slam.
Paints lay scattered at the canvas feet,
The eyes still hang but now they have no one to see.

Zoë Handrill (15)
Kingston Grammar School

Mountain Spirit

White, holding the spirit down
It wears a frown
It's strong
Along the wind travels its song,
Softly singing a quaint little tune,
It hopes to be released some day soon.
The curse of snow is for eternity
It has no time to simply be.
The snow melts down the sunbeams,
This is the subject of all the spirit dreams.
Eternity trapped in spirit
Spirit is trapped in eternity.

Rosalind Axbey (12)
Kingston Grammar School

The Winter Season

The winter season has come again,
summer picnics have been left behind,
no more hot days at the park,
no more laughs on the beach.

The rain has started to freeze,
icicles hang from the frozen roofs,
standing still, not moving, calm.
Patiently waiting for its time to fall.

The lake has now frozen smooth,
people gaze upon the sparkling surface,
remembering their swimming, summer sunshine.
Now it is all behind them, lost, gone.

Cheerful summer faces are a thing of the past,
families huddle together in front of cosy fires,
waiting for the summer, the sun to come again.
They wait and wait but all is lost to the cold.

Nikhil-Raj McDuff (14)
Kingston Grammar School

7am

It's 7am, a cold winter's day, January.
A storm last night left the trees battered and bruised,
Yet still swaying in the cold air.

Frozen gusts, pouring through the open window, whistle in my ear,
Send a cool rush through my body and rush out
Through the wide open window, out of sight.

The cold chimes of the clock tower muffled by the rustle of
Those crisp brown leaves, thrown to the ground by the
Once loved, old, wise trees of centuries past.

The taste of 7am so fresh and clear as I walk
Into the day ahead, I enjoy what's left,
Of that time I love, lost.

Thomas Osborne (14)
Kingston Grammar School

Morning

His dad wakes him up as usual,
And the sunshine through the window,
Causes him to cover up his eyes.

In London, New York and Sydney,
Bright lights carry on beaming,
In the cities that never start sleeping.

The roads are covered in dirt,
The tramps uncurl from their balls like hedgehogs,
And the air fills with early morning coffee from Starbucks.

The London Eye, like a child's Ferris wheel turns,
Seen from all over the land,
Like the sun in the sky.

On Broadway the theatre goers are queuing
Money in their pockets, ready to burn,
Not like Alice in Chains, who awaits her destiny.

The young and hopeless runaways hide,
They used to care and want . . .
Now their hearts are a poor man's pocket.

It's nearing the end of the morning,
The men, late for work, make their blood trickle faster,
Stuck in the traffic, their journey drags on and on, further.

It's the time of day I dislike,
Too quiet and cold, no sense of happiness,
Eyes not quite adjusted to the light,
Make lunch come early, it is the time I most favour.

Huw Procter (14)
Kingston Grammar School

Autumn

The leaves hang, russet brown
from the dusky trees,
Golden, in the evening light
rustling underfoot.

A cool breeze sweeps the town,
bringing with it the birdsong,
And memories of forgotten times
snow glinting on the hills.

The scarlet sun sets,
behind the tower blocks,
As the breeze fades away,
leaving the town behind.

As the late leaves fall,
over the silent town,
The first snow comes drifting down.
Autumn heralds winter.

Abigail King (13)
Kingston Grammar School

Winter

The sharp blade of winter
cuts to the bone.

The land blighted;
bare trees struggle on

Off colour, like the faces
waiting at the bus stop.

Winter catches the throat,
it ensnares the rivers.

Hectic life
frozen still.

Yet hope remains, in dormant buds,
waiting for the healing rays of spring.

Ben Reed (14)
Kingston Grammar School

The Fox

Witty and clever,
cunning and sly,
The sound of traffic
won't turn his eye.

Prowling at night
always aware.
The crack of a twig
and up stands his hair.

Striking his victim,
a quick attack.
Briefly out of the dark
and then he slips back.

Home in the den,
catch dragging behind.
Spies the four cubs
and shows them his find.

Priya Kumar (12)
Kingston Grammar School

War

The sound of gunshot,
The clatter of the trigger,
The smoke from the barrel,
The death from the bullet.

The explosion from a bomb,
The burning of the flames,
The monstrous impact,
The massive recklessness.

The cry of pain,
The blood that is spilt,
The tears that are cried,
The scars that are left.

Andrew Dilmahomed (13)
Kingston Grammar School

Peacekeeper's Daydream

Five fingers
Five minutes.
The bonfires burn and fireworks burst.
On Guy Fawkes Night.

Remember standing around the bonfire,
head tilted upwards,
watching the colours.
The air was frosty.
Now it's all upside down,
and sweat runs down the face.

Two fingers
Two minutes.
The bangs and flashes are the best ever.
But the colours are just reds and orange,
and there are shouts and screams.
On fireworks night.

Funny how history repeats itself,
or not.
Guy Fawkes didn't make it
but we did.

Thirty seconds.
Scared?
Not tonight -
Standby . . .
Standby . . .
Go!

Hugo Johnson (14)
Kingston Grammar School

Street Vibe

Kingston's become my new home town,
So I guess that means it's now time to turn around,
Baggy jeans and skateboards are all you see
Instead of all that Adidas and Nike.
So from Wimbledon tennis that's bat and ball
It's those stumbling telephone boxes,
Let's make that call.

Tomorrow's the weekend,
Let's do something, so it just ain't a dead end.
What d'you have in mind?
Don't be blind, yeah, just tell me.
Let's go and see 'D12' in action, you see
Or do you wanna see a show of 'korn' or 'slipknot'?
I guess I'll just have to watch my evening go to pot.

So Monday's come and first up's history,
Let's get out of bed, bright and early
Cos in da classroom, we're studying World War I.
I just guess that's gonna be - 'gee so much fun'!

The bell rings and it's now four,
I catch da 57 to my own front door.
I'm back to my end, as you can see,
Cos I'm back in my own territory.
After nosh, which you can probably guess is curry -
It's into da bhangra and mc.

Hassan Umarshah (13)
Kingston Grammar School

Waiting For You

I was standing there alone,
in the dark, waiting for you.
Somewhere in my heart,
I had a feeling, a slight hope,
that you would come.

The wind was blowing,
and the night was young.
Everything had gone dark,
with the exception of my heart,
but there was still no change.

My mind had started to wander
in the dreams of us being together.
There was no one stopping us anywhere,
with only us being there.
But the truth, as it always is, bitter
I was still there waiting for you, in vain.

Shirsh Bedi (14)
Kingston Grammar School

Gone!

Like wind you swept me off my feet,
And blew my doubts away.
Like fire you set my heart alight,
And burnt out all the fear.
Like heat your voice, I was so cold,
But my heart began to melt.
I dreamt of you, so sweet and true,
Your touch, your kiss, your stare.
And now you've gone I sit alone,
The tears drop down my cheek.
The rain outside, from way up high,
Falls heavy on your grave.

Holly McDuff (14)
Kingston Grammar School

White Shadows Of Ypres

Soldiers standing in their lines;
In formation on the hill.
Saluting those known only unto God,
In the shadow of an English rose.
Never to know if the war was won;
Or if their sacrifice was in vain.

Regiments are scattered;
The army now united.
They stand forever together,
Among the volunteers and conscripts,
And curious onlookers.
They stand fast and tall.

The place, somewhat defaced,
Not physically, but
By the hoards of schoolchildren,
Breaking the sacred silence.
Polluting the sadness of Tyne Cot.

Ben Siencyn Myers (14)
Kingston Grammar School

Darkness

The wind whistled,
The candle flickered,
An owl swooped overhead.
Looking straight through me as if I was dead,
Silence.

Footsteps
A dim light wavered.
The wind whistled,
The candle flickered,
A twig snapped.
Darkness.

Catherine Dwyer (11)
Kingston Grammar School

Dogs

Dogs can be proud and vicious
Can rip you into shreds
But it seems that my dog Dilbert
Just likes killing flower beds!

A canine chum is what they are
Known as man's best friend
But it seems that my dog Dilbert
Will drive you round the bend!

Once they were just puppies
Just after they were born
But now there is my Dilbert
All my clothes are torn!

Dogs can be good fun
They can also be bad news
But it seems that my dog Dilbert
Gets nutrition from my shoes!

A dog is a big commitment
It can pacify your mood
But I believe that Dilbert
Is just in it for the food!

Edmund Boyd (13)
Kingston Grammar School

Apocolypse

Creeping darkness in the sky
Not a breath, not a sound
The end of the world is nigh.

Suddenly hear Hell's devils cry
Angel chorus all around
Creeping darkness in the sky.

Birds from flaming trees do fly
Dead is the king just crowned
The end of there world is nigh.

Terrified people standing by
Devils grab you tightly bound
Creeping darkness in the sky.

Good people go to Heaven on high
Evil burns below the ground
The end of the world is nigh.

All is gone, no reason why
No footstep, no sound
Creeping darkness in the sky
The end of the world is nigh.

Josi Atkinson (12)
Kingston Grammar School

War

A cool mist settles
Over the bloody field
Dead bodies lay
Forgotten by the ever lengthening
War
Shell holes filled with red water
As the low drone of aircraft
Drive the men mad
And the war still goes on
It was meant to end
At Christmas
But the high command
Was wrong
Now there's even more dead
Forgotten to rot
And still sixty years later
The ghosts walk
Unseen
Haunting the place
Where men lay.

Alex Cannon (13)
Kingston Grammar School

Sssnake

I'm sssomeone, sssomething,
I ssslither and ssslide,
I curve and coil,
I hisss and ssspew,
I wriggle and writhe.

I'm a predator and prey,
I attack and protect,
I ensssnare my victim
Who am I?

I'm sssomeone, sssomething!

Karla Bennett (13)
Kingston Grammar School

In The Muddy Trenches

Shallow pits of murky water,
Deep darkness never-ending.
Rusty barbed wire coiling us in,
To the dank dugout where we hunch on cold nights,
And where rotting bodies lay
Motionless.

Rats scamper over the rotting bodies,
I feel soulless just looking at them.
My unwashed hair tangled with cobwebs,
My gashes and pores clogged with dirt,
Squelchy mud, pushing away
Thoughts of family and home.

Anna Stevenson (13)
Kingston Grammar School

Barbed Wire

It is as deadly as a field of thorns,
Glistening with raindrops,
In the early morning sun.
Coiled round the muddy ditch of a battlefield,
Like a giant spider's web.
It looks so harmless, just sitting there,
Waiting for its prey.
Then minutes later, hundreds of
Bodies thrown over it.
Like a huge washing line.
Draining red water
From the already bloodstained corpses.

Jonathan Gray (13)
Kingston Grammar School

Try Again

The tears trickle from your eyes,
You've lost!
Was it because of you -
You wonder?
Was it that missed conversion?
Missed opportunity?
The other team were just better,
You hope you're right.
Are you worthy of your club's badge?
Does your team really need you?
'Great run, you were on fire!'
Or was the coach just being kind?
You go home, caked in mud,
Your limbs ache.
Your body's bruised from all those deadly tackles,
Then all night you have flashbacks.
Could you have done better?
'Son, it wasn't your fault!'
Your mother's kindness consoles you.
You fall asleep, truly beaten,
To fight another day.

Theo Franklinos (14)
Kingston Grammar School

Dolphins

They've been my best friends all my life
They only play and have fun
They break the water like a knife.

Capricorn starred in Jaws 3
And I had such fun with thee
They've been my best friends all my life.

He sings so sweet on command
And does a flip or two
And he breaks the water like a knife.

I was only with him two hours
But it's a memory I'll never forget
He's been my best friend all my life.

As he dives out of the water
It is a magnificent scene
He breaks the water like a knife.

He did not want me to leave
He tried to swim after me,
He breaks the water like a knife
They've been my best friends, all my life.

Matthew Parker (12)
Kingston Grammar School

Rats

Prolific breeder
Screeching squealer,
Vicious vermin
Disease carrier.
Plague spreader,
Sewer scurrier.
Solitary scavenger,
Black devil.
Agile creeper,
Razor-fanged biter.
Omnivorous nibbler,
Loathsome creature.
Whiskered fiend,
Despised rodent.
A dirty rat!

Will Cannell (13)
Kingston Grammar School

Free Verse

Sometimes
I wish I could turn back time,
On the awful things I've said
On the stupid things I've done,
On the cruel things I've thought.

Sometimes
I wish I could speed up time,
To a sunny, summer holiday,
To a crispy, white Christmas,
To a sparkling Bonfire Night.

Sometimes,
I like time just the way it is.

Beth Oddy (12)
Kingston Grammar School

Queen Of The Ocean

Majestic in her loneliness
Trapped in an oblivion of gloom,
Perched above the water's edge,
She's the queen of sailor's doom.

Her blackened skirts spread beneath the waves,
To entice unwitting souls,
The beauty of her glacial smile,
Protects a heart of callous coal.

A snow maiden on icy horizons,
She's a sentinel of Arctic realms.
Surrender is their only choice,
For she will never be overwhelmed.

A goddess of bitter oceans,
Magnificent to behold.
Passing into her eternity
Her thrilling embrace is forever cold.

Georgia Ford (13)
Kingston Grammar School

Drop

Falling, falling,
Falling, falling.
As I fall from the sky
From up on high.
Why do I fall, why don't I fly?
I want to free myself, you see.
Captivated by the air, it makes me wonder
Why can I never change?
Will I ever roam, where I want or don't?
Will I ever swiftly fly,
Through the lake into the bed?
Down, down, ever down.
Down, down, never down.

Roger Hamilton-Martin (13)
Kingston Grammar School

The River

Lively young stream, bubbling down the mountain,
Bounding past trees, flinging itself off small cliffs.
Clear, pure, ice cold shallows,
Running frantically downwards.
A wild, sloshing mess.

Gradually it becomes deeper,
Sliding more quietly past windswept fields.
Like a long, winding snake,
A ribbon, weaving through the landscape.

The murky, dark depths of the mature river,
Flowing into bustling towns, then polluted cities.
The river, now wise with the knowledge of its journey,
Joins the vast power of the rumbling sea.

Sophie Dyer (13)
Kingston Grammar School

Death

He creeps effortlessly, silently and with hate,
He has seen horrors so great that would make your gut churn.
He has lost all sense of time and age,
He has lost all sense of fear and reason.
He has no mercy, you can make no deal,
For when you meet him, the road ends.
When you meet him, you look into those empty eyes,
And then you understand death,
And when you understand death, you understand life.
And in that brief second, before you end known life,
You will laugh or cry,
You may be going to Heaven, you may be going to Hell,
You may be going nowhere, but I assure you
Death means the *end!*

Rowan Hunter (14)
Kingston Grammar School

Three Words

Three simple words cannot begin
To describe the way I feel about you.

From the moment you stepped into my life,
You became everything to me.
My being, my existence.
When I look into your eyes
I travel to the depths of your soul
And say a million things
Without any trace of sound.
I can picture the way your tears
Make me want to change the world,
So that it doesn't hurt you anymore.
You know that my own life is
Inexorably consumed within
The beating of your very heart.
I love you for a million reasons,
No paper, prose or poem could do it justice.
Three simple words, one profound meaning.

Georgina Hulland Brown (13)
Kingston Grammar School

Cross Fire

Cross after cross, lying motionless,
    Each one a window to the past.
A scene of endless fighting,
    Of shells striding past, like chariots of death.
Each bullet wedded to a victim,
    Images of death and suffering.
Of disease and pain,
    Of gas squeezing life out of a soldier.
Until the window creaks shut,
    A cross remains -
        A man, lost to history.

Adam Tomas Krolak (13)
Kingston Grammar School

Troubles

As I step upon the golden grains of sand with
my board in hand.
I look out to sea and think about the troubles
left behind me.
The wind blows, but no one knows about the
troubles that go when you're by the sea.

The sun beats down, a man frowns at me,
staring into space,
I quickly make haste and throw myself into the sea,
Hours past but this feeling must last
as the sun now sets upon a trouble-free world.

Lights begin to appear upon the beach and I
realise that the day's not done
But there is still fun for at least one more
hour, to come.

This hour has passed, my day is done,
The trouble-free day is gone
and it's back to a trouble ridden world.

James Treen (14)
Kingston Grammar School

Acne

Bulging red and yellow pimples
Like moon craters full of puss
I try to squeeze them to death
But they are indestructible, they just won't die
Constant itchy, grease all over my face
Like thousands of aliens, growing on me
The horror on people's faces tells me about the horror on mine
Full of flaky, facial crust
Waiting to explode like a volcano
No more am I that cute little blond boy.

Sam Marchant (13)
Kingston Grammar School

They Call Me Evil

A piercing scream
A thousand daggers
A cold, black shadow
Black soot, burnt ash

I made fear,
I made unhappiness
How did I start?
No one has a clue.
When will I die?
Never.

I am eternal hatred
Watch out
I could take you over,
No one ever knows where I am
Or where I'm heading.
I'm a red-eyed cat,
Swift and skilful.

I'm in a deep, deep pit
Hidden under leaves, in a dark, dark forest
Anyone could fall into me
I can turn anyone to destruction,
Take them over, control them
Every move they make.

A piercing scream
A thousand daggers
A cold, black shadow
Black soot, burnt ash.

They call me Evil.

Tanya Barth (12)
Kingston Grammar School

Anorexia

Anorexia for me is a burden of despair,
I state it as being immensely unfair.
Each human that can stay healthy without worry,
A miracle-maker. Superman in action.

It controls me, my thoughts, my mind,
The outcome's unpleasant and unkind.
All I ask for is an amiable life
In this lifetime is happiness, for which I must strive.
Becoming without worry, seems too far to believe,
With the pessimistic thoughts running up my sleeve.

To the outside world, it is somewhat invisible,
It is difficult to explain, it is inexplicable.
In disguise, it's comprised of miniature Hitlers,
Taking over my mind.
Like a thief it prowls in and out of my conscience.
I am my own prisoner, this is complete nonsense.

For I know each individual has their good and bad in life,
My good was my achievements, my studies, my sports;
My bad was my family, no my thoughts or being gaunt.

I long for one singular wish,
Not for a huge, three-paged list.
Is that really too much to ask -
In my prior life, was my spirit that dark?

Food gets checked, weighed and measured
To eat something different, I'd feel greatly pressured
Life's hard to get by with the one I love most,
Conflicts with my mum, she's a horrible ghost.

I ask for help, yell, plead
They inform me that it's on its way!
Yet I wait solitary, day by day!

Kunal Patel (12)
Kingston Grammar School

The Rider

Upon a lonely clifftop, a clearing in the trees,
Stood a night-black horse, upon which sat its rider,
Her black cloak billowing in the breeze.
All around there was silence, everything was still
When suddenly, the horse reared up, neighing high and shrill,
It tore through the forest of bare trees which gave a haunted look,
It raced over frosty leaves and stumbled in an icy brook.
They went on cantering through the night, when they came to a halt.
They stood facing a towering door with a rusty keyhole and bolt.
The door belonged to a castle which dwelt in those lonely mountains,
It now stood silent and empty.
They say it's cursed - causes suffering and pain to all men.
The rider hid amongst the shadows in the courtyard,
When the charcoal-grey clouds parted and moved,
So that silver moonlight slanted down, revealing
The rider, the horse pawing the ground with its hooves.
The rider pulled a hood over her head, veiling and hiding her pale face,
And she moved again to hide once more in the shadows
Of that cursed and enchanted place.
Her intense green eyes glared at the air above the door,
An arrow, tense in her bow, poised, pointing at the cobbled floor.
But whomever she was waiting for, never dared to show.
So she rode into the forest's darkness,
Her hair whipped from her face, her eyes searching for her foe.

Anna Steinitz (12)
Kingston Grammar School

Seasons

Spring
The spring bud opens,
Flowering beauty spreads
A light after the storm.

Summer
The young fire shimmers,
Unfolding summer blooms,
A leap into the light.

Autumn
The cold hand reaches,
Flowering spirit dies
The light fading away.

Winter
The white void rises,
Engulfing summer ends,
Its death as first snow falls.

James Henderson (11)
Kingston Grammar School

The Sea

A clash
The great archangel of water
The sea
A power unknown
Jumping, breathing, living
Whatever you can do.
Ultimately she prevails.
The player of the lands
Like a huge drumbeat
The sea plays here
Is silent there
Ever seeing
Ever playing
The rhythm stays and stays and stays.

Stephanie Swan (13)
Kingston Grammar School

Think!

*(Dedicated to those who have honourably
lost their lives in Iraq)*

Have you ever seen
A man die in front of your eyes?
Hear him yell in pain
Before he dies?

Have you ever heard
A man scream and groan?
Hear his soul
Before his skin turns to stone?

Have you ever felt
A man die in your hands?
Feel him go limp
Even his hair strands?

Have you ever smelled
A man die in your sight?
The foul stench of death
Fighting for his country, in a lost fight?

Have you ever thought
You were that man
Dying for no reason?
Change it, you can.

Tom Quilter (12)
Kingston Grammar School

The Butterfly

As it glides through the air,
I watch its symmetrical wings fly,
It soars through the sky like a bird,
Landing on a flowerbed peacefully.

I listen to the beat of its heart,
Tiny but powerful.
I admire its wonderful choice of colours,
Like a sun standing out among the rest.

It's raining now,
And every colour on the flowers are drowned out by the rain.
But my butterfly still has its colours and is still here,
Standing powerful amongst the rest.

It's symmetrical wings inspire me,
No one notices these creatures
They camouflage themselves to suit their liking of being unnoticed
And only if we recognised these creatures
Maybe we'd notice their beauty.

Estelle Khajenouri (12)
Kingston Grammar School

The Horse

Free spirit that goes over hill and dale,
Running wild as the stormy sea.
Exploring with our Creator's gale
Exceptional is this galloping beast!

Whilst moving with that Creator's cares
It is known as nature's best.
Like to the cheetahs, like to the hares - with
Distance and amazing speed.

Beauty and grace, solemn and sure,
Every head turns, starts and stares.
So fast, so fleet, so noble and pure,
The horse, God's creation, the best.

Francesca Rodger (12)
Kingston Grammar School

The Order Was Given . . .

The order was given for the battle to commence
It was like all the furies of Hell,
Each soldier's aim was to keep their defence
But still with no choice, some men fell.

They all made sure they were aware of their rear
As they shot down the Germans,
There existed no word such as fear
The battlefield was not a sight for humans.

The battle slowly started to cease
As the Germans could no longer repel,
The soldiers started to ease
As the Germans completely fell.

The soldiers returned home as patriots
To their long-awaited children and wife.
There is no longer any riots
So the soldiers can enjoy a peaceful life.

Eric Finton-James (14)
Kingston Grammar School

Bats

Creatures of the night,
Black, furry, cave lovers,
Ferocious, deadly, ugly, they go up for height,
Creatures of the night!

Creatures of the night,
Sensitive, warm, darkness junkies,
Stealthy, accurate, blood drainers ready for the bite,
Creatures of the night!

Creatures of the night,
Blind as a bat,
Just trying to hide from the light,
Creatures of the night!

Peter Harrison (12)
Kingston Grammar School

The Owl

It waits patiently,
A small rustle in a hedge,
The predator's attention is focused
On the movement beneath the ledge.

Small rodents,
All kinds, it scares
They all rush to hide,
Trying to avoid its evil glares.

A twitch of the head
And the spotlight is moved,
A new victim has been announced
The one in the deep groove.

The small mouse
Has made a mistake,
It moves from the reeds
Beside the lake.

The owl's eyes watch carefully,
Waiting for one more shake
To confirm his choice.
Or is it a fake?

The prey doesn't dare move,
Its destiny lies
Only
In its predator's beady eyes.

There it was,
The proof it had been waiting for,
The owl moves swiftly
Towards the floor.

The elegant attacks have stopped,
The mouse no longer stirs
But the owl is not fulfilled
It needs another taste of fur.

Sophie Salmon (13)
Kingston Grammar School

My Cat

Prowling around
Slinking along
Waving his tail
His jumping is strong

Catching a mouse
Holding it high
Anything edible
He wants to try

In daytime he is peaceful
At night, on the prowl
His cat eyes - bright green
And sharp as an owl

He eats a lot
But never gets fat
Always out searching
For that illusive rat

He still has nine lives
At least that's what I think
Although I am not
A feline shrink!

He's a tabby
And a cool cat for sure
Yes I have had him
Since I was four.

Barney Leach (12)
Kingston Grammar School

Open Your Eyes

Open your eyes, what can you see -
Steam rising from a cup of tea?
The red English rose
Beneath your nose.
Waving in the air the Queen's white glove,
As gentle and graceful as a dove.
Stonehenge and The Angel Of The North,
What else can England bring forth?

A silver Aston Martin, driving by your house,
When you are missing cheddar, you blame the mouse.
Shakespeare plays are not forgotten,
English prices here are rotten.
Greasy food and dirty street
Posh old people, you may meet.
Wipe those tears off your face
England isn't such a bad place.

England is a rich and prosperous location,
Many people come here on vacation.
The London Eye stands proud
Above the gathering crowd.
Buckingham Palace and Big Ben
English cricket teams have lost again.
The countryside, the foaming sea
Open your eyes and this is what you'll see.

Hadrien Soldati (12)
Kingston Grammar School

War

You never thought about the next day,
Only whether you would survive *this* day.
They were just normal people like me,
Thinking the same as me.
I stood alone, a body without a soul,
My mind, embroiled in a bitter struggle over right and wrong.

I stand there smiling, embracing the new found freedom,
The wisdom of life that sleep evermore, awakens inside me,
A burning spirit wanting to avenge fallen comrades from the past.
A river once blocked, now reaches out and touches the sea.

I stood there feeling patriotic,
Waiting for the order to go over the top!
I was going to do my bit for my country.
Rifle in one hand and knife in the other,
John and I chatted about home,
That was the last time I ever spoke to him.

Our trench was hit,
I was luckier than most.
Some were hit a small bit
Some where burned, like toast,
Some were killed
And the Germans were thrilled.

All these years later
I think . . . and think again,
What was the reason?
My fallen comrades, forever gone.
War for me is a sin.

Benjamin Skliar-Ward (13)
Kingston Grammar School

The City Of The Damned

On the breeze, the faint echo of your voice,
Your name is at the tip of my tongue,
My thoughts are dominated by your face,
The pain you have caused has bounded me here,
In the city of the damned.

Observing up and down the deep, black sky,
My past, my pain is written in the stars,
But they won't shine for me,
They won't guide me out of my darkness,
Lost.

It's a carious wasteland, death's backyard,
His stench overcomes all other senses,
But life exists, lost souls searching for an exit,
Although my sight isn't failing,
Reality tells me they are deceiving me.

I have created an ocean with my tears,
I'm confused, I shouldn't be here,
But you've destroyed my sanity,
All alone to pick up the pieces,
With my bloodstained hands.

Demons have released, they're torturing me,
Preparing me like a main course,
Tenderising my soul, ready for breakdown,
I'm powerless to them, they're ignoring my screams,
They will only answer to you.

My eyes have dried, like an empty well,
I cannot fight anymore,
I'm waiting for you,
In the city of the damned.

Naseer Hayath (13)
Kingston Grammar School

The Stranger

The stranger looks at you
with deep, meaningful eyes,
colours changing: blue grey, green.
What is she thinking?
What does she feel?
You want to ask,
but what words to say?
Chin quivers lips tense,
and a tear falls out of a saddened eye.
A strand of hair slips out of place
and shrouds a sad, painful face.
You want to call her
tell her to stay
but she turns away
into a sea of unknown faces.
Swept on a wave of futile confusion.
Drowning in an ocean of misinterpretation.
Stop! Come back!
But the voice never reaches and
the sound is never heard.
Meaning lost in unsaid phrases.
If only she knew . . .
that stranger is you!

Kezia Evans (13)
Kingston Grammar School

Goldfish

Goldfish darting in the weeds,
Floating in the dark and deep.
Gliding backwards and forwards,
Slowly drifting into each other's keep.

Brightly coloured,
The gold, dorsal fin.
Flaps to and fro
Vibrating the back of the skin.

Murky areas,
Herons see a gold glint,
Polluted waters
Give them a big hint.

The heron strikes
And as the fish is about to die
Floating, unsuspended,
Thinking how it's been living a lie.

Graham Davies (12)
Kingston Grammar School

Whispering Reeds

A Broad's yacht
Sweeping gracefully past abandoned windmills
Her tanned sails, luffing in the light air
White hull slipping through the murky water.

Water lapping on her hull
Swans' wings beating in the sky
And the cry of the Marsh Harrier
The boom creaks under the strain.

Eel traps set by bearded fishermen
Reed cutters working silently on the bank
A Wherry passing the starboard bow
Homeward-bound for Horning.

Toby Mumford (13)
Kingston Grammar School

Cats

We come in all shapes and sizes
and some of us even win prizes.
Our fur can be short or long
and at night, we can sing an awful song.
We are a pet for both young and for old,
but we do not like being out in the cold.
Feed us and treat us right,
and we promise never to fight or bite.
Our favourite food is fish
and possibly roast beef if you wish.
We wander freely as we need
unlike dogs who need a lead.
We will purr and show affection when stroked,
but be mean and we'll need to be coaxed.
We may spit and scratch
if you come on our home patch.
Mice and birds are what we chase
but dogs are our worst case.
We sleep for twenty hours a day,
not a bad life, I hear you say!

Sarah Burnham (11)
Kingston Grammar School

Oxshott Heath

A thick carpet of purple heather on the floor.
A stairway of squelchy mud leads up to a landing of pine cones.
A canopy of branches tower over me.
The bright leaves form a window to the clear blue sky.
I lie on a bed of prickly pine needles listening to the birdsong.
The breeze on a cool summer's day blows my face, I smell fresh air.
I sit on a comforting sofa of sweet smelling flowers
And watch the squirrels scrabbling up the trees,
Trying to find crunchy acorns.

The heath is my home.

Emily Galazka (12)
Manor House School

Little Brothers

Little brothers are like slimy newts,
Covered in slime,
And very small!

They can howl,
They can scream,
It's their way of getting whatever they want!

They have millions of toys scattered around,
Which are never picked up,
Just left on the ground!

Constant trips to McDonald's,
Toy shops, funfairs and playgrounds,
Constant buying of sticky lollipops!

Screaming tantrums,
Slamming doors,
No peace at night, and more!

It's time for revenge,
So when they're fast asleep,
We crawl into their rooms
And . . .
Wake them up!

Victoria Browne (12)
Manor House School

Painting

When the sun is shining brightly through the window,
That is when I love to paint,
I love to paint in different seasons,
And plenty of scenes.

I love to paint in autumn time with all the fluttering, falling leaves,
With all the beautiful burning red colours,
I love to paint my colourful garden,
And the crooked trees.

I love to paint in winter with snow on the ground,
With prickly holly wreaths on doors,
I love to paint the people with their woolly hats,
And fantastic glittering Christmas trees.

I love to paint in springtime,
The vivid colours of flowers,
I love to paint gaily-patterned Easter eggs,
And fresh green grass.

I love to paint in summer,
The burning beaches,
And tanned excited people,
I love to paint my family,
In the bright sunlight.

Emily Cannon (12)
Manor House School

Birds And Seasons

Early morning blackbirds sing at sunrise,
Woodpeckers are hammering their holes in dead wood,
The distant call of the cuckoo,
Spring is here.

Baby birds just learning to fly,
Swooping swallows feeding on the wing,
Skylarks singing out of sight,
Summer brings a surprise.

Migrating birds moving southwards,
Canadian geese squawking at dusk,
Hovering hawks getting their talons ready as killing machines,
Autumn is arriving.

The red-breasted robin sits on the gate in the snow,
Blue tits and sparrows picking and pecking at the frozen ground,
Mossy nests in holly hedgerows; birds are biting the berries,
Winter is awaiting.

Rebecca Fellowes-Freeman (12)
Manor House School

Swimming

As the clear, cold water laps against my feet, I pull on my
blue goggles.
I dive under, powering through the deep.
My arms pull back, my legs kicking up and down.

People push past me to pick up the brightly coloured rings
on the blue bottom.
I float on my back, looking up at a cloudless sky.
Voices echoing behind me, loud and excited.

Splash! I'm covered with droplets of water.
As they throw themselves in, landing on bellies.

The smell of chlorine makes me feel dizzy.
I climb out and towel my wet body dry.

Mary Flynn (13)
Manor House School

Why You?

Why I can't say
I love you.
Why I dream about you
And I can't sleep.
Why I am cross
When you smile to another.
Why I think about you all the time,
About your eyes and how you smile.
Why when I look to the stars
I am thinking about you.

Your smile
Like a baby.
Sweet kiss
Like a chocolate.
Feeling warm
In my heart,
Like a volcano coming here.
Don't make me jealous
Or hurt me.
Love doesn't hurt.
It makes me and you
Love forever.

Yes, I love you
But why I can't say it.
Why I can't say
I love you.
Why?

Wafa Hussein (13)
Manor House School

Country Lanes

Walk along the lanes, a wonderful place to be,
Colours, sounds and smells mark the changes of seasons.

Leaves become red, yellow, orange and brown,
Floating slowly down, catch one if you can!
Squirrels scurry, collecting nuts to hoard,
Blackberries and sloes hang juicy and ripe.
It is autumn in the lanes.

Leaves crackle underfoot as you walk peacefully,
Frosty, bare treetops are stark against the grey sky.
Cotton wool covers the mammoth plain fields,
Snow and hail overhead patters down hard.
It is winter in the lanes.

Animals love this time of year, lambs skip, rabbits burrow,
Flowers bloom as the trees blossom in moist air.
Birds find nesting twigs in the hedgerow,
Fields are light green and sprouting slowly.
It is spring in the lanes.

The trickle of a stream running along nearby,
As the barley sways gently to and fro.
Animals shelter under shady-covered trees,
The sun beams down on the glimmering fields.
It is summer in the lanes.

Emma Crook (12)
Manor House School

Family

'Ow! Mum, he pulled my hair!'
'You liar, I never did!'
'Go to your room, both of you!'
It's only 7.30 on a Sunday,
And guess what, I'm woken up again,
By screaming and wailing, shouting and crying.
That's my little brother and sister.

'But I want to watch football!'
'I was here first!'
'Be quiet, Becky's asleep!'
I wish.
I snuggle down in my covers,
But I can't block out the sound,
Of screaming and wailing, shouting and crying.
Oh please, I have school tomorrow.

'I had the milk first!'
'No you did not!'
'You'll both go without in a sec.'
I'd better go downstairs,
But I don't want to meet,
The screaming and wailing, shouting and crying.
On second thoughts, there'll be no milk left.

'Hey! He pushed me!'
'You kicked me first!'
'Good morning, Becky, dear.'
I grab a bowl and spoon,
And start to eat, but still it goes on:
The screaming and wailing, shouting and crying.
Will it never stop?

Rebecca McGee (12)
Manor House School

The Sea

The ever-changing colours of a water wonderland
Expands to the horizon and beyond,
The wind rises: the waves wash and dance,
It falls: they sink still, settled and serene.
The hidden treasures underneath, waiting for their unveiling
Are revealed when the tide goes out, like opening a safe of jewels.
Again the wind slaps her face
Whipping water into a frenzy,
Churning the white crests into galloping horses.
Yet, far away, the sea is a tranquil mirror.

Katie Fieldman (12)
Manor House School

Drifting In The Shade

Rain drips down the back of your neck under trees,
Dirt clings to your unwashed feet.
The only part of you that is clean on this night,
Are the tracks tears left on your cheeks.

Last night I dreamed again. Of you.
My mind only sees things in pretend.
The dream was still sad; your tears still were real
Yet everything comes to an end.

You're so beautiful it hurts me to think
How precious you are to me,
I know you won't be there when I wake
But don't say you'll ever leave.

So peaceful, but I feel an aching inside
And I don't listen, for the life is fled,
I know. You are gone, love . . .
You are more than dead.

Ashes of the words, they haunt my tongue.
And I close my eyes against wind overhead.
You are so gone, love,
So much more than dead.

Amy Leonard (17)
Lingfield Notre Dame Senior School

From The Revolutions Of The Wheels On My Chair

Everybody's talking about the breaking chains,
I only hear the muffled voices,
As if they were speaking through clenched teeth.
The lost soul of an unshaven, scruffy face,
Told me about it.

The chains bent and curved with such ease,
As the beast writhed and wriggled.
It escaped, like I want to,
Away from the stifled intonation of lost, unshaven souls,
And the beasts of untold fairy tales.

Sometimes I'd sit and watch a movie,
A horror film with a similar beast.
I hide away from the scary parts,
But know I could never run away,
For my wheels restrict my motion.

I sit by French doors alone at night.
I look out upon the moonlit undergrowth.
The beast is out there, lurking, waiting for me.
The unshaven souls don't know the power of the beast,
That keeps me from my night-time slumber.

I can feel the presence of dangerous power,
Even now in my bed, the unshaven one's words still shake me.
Clash! It gently gripped and grabbed the stairs.
Creak! I cannot move, so my eyes search the darkness. Nothing.

I'm out with my friends shopping, *walking*, having fun.
I'm in a dream, an amazing memory.
Another clash! Is it in my mind? I ignore it.
Yet another, so I crawl to my chair, eyes closed in fear.
And once in my chair I open my eyes,
To perceive the dangerous power of the beast.

Alanya Holder (14)
Lingfield Notre Dame Senior School

Despair

His shoulders are hunched, his head in his hands -
He is alone.

He sees not the light around him,
Only the darkness that engulfs his soul -
He is alone.

Though the night is warm,
He shivers and shakes
From the cold that chills his heart -
He is alone.

He moans and he cries, but nobody hears him -
For he is alone.

He hears not the chirping of the birds,
Only the funeral bells in his head -
For he is alone.

Though some say life is sweet,
Madness takes over him, fear
From the doom that he knows is his

For he is alone in a cruel, dark world -
A world that does not care.

Mark Attree (13)
Lingfield Notre Dame Senior School

Anger

Anger is a loud shout and an annoyance.
It is a tear falling down someone's face.
Everybody is yelling and there are things
Happening that shouldn't happen.

Everyone is full of anger - shouting and crying.
They all look angry - irritated eyes, an upset
Expression on their faces, tears rolling down
Their faces and hatred inside them.

Abigail Teece (14)
Prior's Field School

Fear

The girl is afraid,
Afraid of the past
She tries to remember,
But the thought did not last.

It happened not long ago
From this day.
But nobody knows,
Why she moved away.

Whatever did happen?
That tormenting hour.
Something took over,
Some kind of power.

The girl is afraid,
Afraid from this day.
But nobody knows,
Why she moved away.

Ruth Welton (13)
Prior's Field School

Beauty Is . . .

Beauty is a word I don't understand,
I think it's to do with the touch of the hand,
Maybe the way you move to the side,
Maybe the way you look me in the eye,
Beauty is a word I don't understand.

Is it fear?
Is it sorrow?
Here today, gone tomorrow.

Beauty is a word you can't understand,
I think it's special, I do not know . . .
For beauty is a word I can't understand!

Emma Lamden (12)
Prior's Field School

Grief

I stand alone,
Green should be in front of me,
But instead,
A white field with specks of green grass,
Climbing up the sides of the white crosses.

Underneath,
Brave soldiers are buried.
The graves stretch for miles,
It's like a film,
But this is real.

People have suffered,
People have died.
Blood has been shed
And families have cried.

I stand there alone,
On the hill,
I know I'm alone,
But I can hear voices,
Not in my head,
But around me,
I catch a word,
Over and over again,
No, no, no
And then screams,
Screams that make my ears ache,
Screams that mean that another has died.

Then silence again.
Rain.
I'm soaking,
I don't know how long I have been here,
But I am soaked to the bone,
Thunder roars and lightning strikes,
Forking across the dark sky.

I look once more upon the battlefield,
Then turn and walk away,
A tear trickling down my already wet cheek,
I leave,
Never to see this site again,
The site where so many men,
Lost their precious lives.

Rebecca Thomas (13)
Prior's Field School

Loneliness

The girl is sitting on the swing.
There is a large, glistening tear inside her,
hanging there, waiting to fall,
to spill over and break her down.
Her smiling face is a glossy mask,
for underneath it is raw, true unhappiness.
The memories, missed opportunities,
good and bad, sweet and sour,
half and half, battling to get out.
Life before was taken for granted,
all that was good gone,
the realisation is sharp.
A tiny flower in the garden,
strangely all alone,
across from a crowded patch of colour.
Being alone, the odd one out,
is no new feeling.
The girl picks the flower and walks away.
And left alone, gently propelled back and forth by the wind,
bunches of autumn leaves billowing about, is the empty swing.

Emily Baxter (13)
Prior's Field School

Loneliness

She sits in her living room gazing into space,
On her pink leather sofa covered with lace.
Her name is Geraldine, but nobody cares
She has just lost her husband, one half of a pair.

She does have a daughter, but they argued years ago
Since then she has been feeling emotionally low.
She thinks of times gone by and remembers an old bike,
A straw hat, a red biscuit tin,
She stares at the television, not taking anything in.

There is a knock at the door. She rushes, wonders who it is
But there is no one there,
She looks and can see a group of giggling kids
She goes into the kitchen and makes a cup of tea.
She looks at the telephone, should she ring and see?

She picks up the receiver and dials the numbers carefully
It's ringing. Now there's no going back, she waits hopefully.
There is an answer! 'Hello, oh wait a second, I'm just reading a note.'
Geraldine can't say anything. Her voice is stuck in her throat.

'Hello, is anybody there? Argh! This damn phone
I bet we need a new one, I should've known!'
Geraldine opens her mouth to say something,
She had a million things to say to her daughter only last week
Click . . . 'The other person has hung up.'
Beep, beep, beep!

Tahnee Atkin (13)
Prior's Field School

Sadness

There is a house, it's dark and silent.
There is a girl indoors mourning lost love
As innocent as a child, as sweet as a dove

The lights are off, the doors are creaking
She's all alone, she won't be sleeping

She shuts her eyes and remembers a dream
Of a magical land where her love has been

He won't be back, he's now the past
But her love for him will always last

The house so quiet, she can hear him talking,
His laughter, his love and the fun days walking.

She remembers his face, his lips, his eyes
She grips her pillow, lies down and sighs

No goodbye he's gone forever
Happiness over, no longer together

He calls to her beyond the grave
Her life she does not wish to save

It's time to end this life of pain
And join her lover once again

She takes the poison to her bed
When morning comes the girl is dead

The end is sad, a tale of woe
But life and death were ever so.

Gabriella Baranowska (13)
Prior's Field School

Grief

Carmen sits in a room
Her face sodden and blotched.
She gazes into the warm fire and wishes she was there,
Then she remembers something
She becomes more fixated
And she remembers her mother.

Her name was Scarlet;
Long, fiery-red hair
Wispy yet thick!
She had dark, smoky eyes
And pale skin.

Carmen remembers a picnic they shared,
Not long ago in a field with trees sparsely placed.
They had an argument you see, Carmen ran off,
In a terrible rage Scarlet could not see her daughter,
Here nor there, Carmen saw from behind a tree,
Her mother run into the road, *a scream! A squeal of brakes.*

Carmen sits and weeps at her mother's death,
She cries herself a waterfall of guilt and pain.
'It was my fault,' she says to herself, 'my fault!'
The fire gave a final spark and died.

Jess Devenish (13)
Prior's Field School

Thundering Hooves

The sound of the thundering hooves,
Is so soothing as we canter,
Faster, faster we go,
Along the sandy beach,
Watching the sun go down
And then we stop,
I am sad
Sad that this day could not last longer.

Megan Nixon (11)
Prior's Field School

Loneliness

An abandoned dog in the woods,
No one is calling him.
Alone, lost, terrified,
Looking all around for the family or an exit.

No warm bedding to curl up in,
Or Aga to lean against,
Just the touch of the cold, wet undergrowth,
In a place that leads to nowhere.

Feeling intimidated,
The wild animals rush around to find a nice, cosy bed,
The night is drawing in and stars fill the sky,
The noises of the night are all around.

Huddled in a ball,
Safe from the incomplete prods of daggers,
Only to hear the moans
And he groans from the animals.

Alice Lougee (14)
Prior's Field School

Is It . . .

Is it now that I become a woman
And if not, when?

Is it when I get my first crush,
Is it then?

Or is it when my heart has broken,
After first touching true love?

After being denied that wonderful gift
Some believe is from above.

Or is there no real turning point?
No sudden moment of clarity?

Perhaps we are always a woman and always a child
And always full of frivolity?

Nicole Adam (12)
Prior's Field School

50 Years

Slam went the big oak door,
The two curious children entered the house.
It was so dark they could not see the floor,
They wandered round, then got bored.
So went back to the big oak door,
They tried to leave, but it would not open.

Fifty years they kept on trying and trying the door,
Something possessed them, they didn't eat, they didn't sleep.
They kept on trying and trying.

Suddenly, one day the children gave a cry,
The big oak door opened wide.
The children took a step outside,
They suddenly aged.
Sixty-one they were all wrinkled and old.
They were hungry and thirsty and went home,
Where their mother would be waiting arms open.
Where their house once stood was a motorway.

They asked people where they were,
These people were rude and did not care,
Or was it that the once curious children had died?

Harriet Pelling (12)
Prior's Field School

The Bullies

They threw me in a crumpled heap,
Upon the floor I lay,
Motionless and twitching,
I tried to creep away.
They kicked me back and glared at me
And showed me a metal gun,
I trembled and shouted, 'No!'
Too late it was already done.

Phoebe Thompson (13)
Prior's Field School

Books!

Books, books, they'll never go
They'll never fade
They'll make your knowledge grow
All the time I'm reading
I'm in my own little world
I know so much I'll soon be leading
The honour scholars at Harvard Law
And then when I'm Prime Minister
I will do so much including stopping war
If more people read more books
Their IQs will soar
They'll learn about so much more
Sometimes about crooks
I love reading non fiction or fiction
Romance, comedy or sadness
Reading always causes friction
With me!

Holly Graham-Wood (12)
Prior's Field School

Trying

One day they'll say,
She's always trying, trying, trying,
Trying to do her best,
Trying not to make a mess,
Trying to make the best flower bunch,
Trying to do the best karate punch,
Trying always to munch her lunch,
Trying not to be lazy,
Trying to do the best for her friend Daisy,
Trying always to be kind,
Trying to have a good mind,
Always trying, trying, trying.

Jessica Littlewood (11)
Prior's Field School

Euridice

The water was calm, the trees still.
He broke my peace.
With force and aggression,
Cracking the silence like a whip,
Catching the air in its grasp, as he did me.
I fled.

Running and running,
The fear gushed through my veins.
Then I stumbled,
As I felt a sharp pain.
I looked to where I had stepped and saw it.
The snake was the last thing I looked upon.

Hell.
That was the only word for it.
Lost souls, screaming
To loved ones.
And he came.
Came for me, boldly through
The darkness, with no fear.

My hope rose to the dark skies,
My faith sprang back to life,
As if it had been dormant.
And I followed him,
So happy, yet so scared, praying,
Don't look back.

And we kept on.
Every step one inch closer to life,
And the fear one bit lighter,
Just praying and then suddenly, we saw the end,
He walked out into the sun and
I was so relieved.

Then I saw him turning. I was shouting
But there was no sound.
Fear flooded through me as if
A dam had burst.
The familiar screaming,
The pain, starting in my head again.
I was lost.

Catherine Lenain (13)
Prior's Field School

Joyfulness

Gleaming, white sparkly teeth,
With large green eyes and a few brown freckles.
Butterflies gliding in the park,
The sun is shining and all is well.

Always laughing, unforgettable
Like my godmother, never stops.
She keeps on skipping with a smile on her face,
The horse in the distance, clippity clops.

It bubbles up inside you,
Until they get larger and are finally set free,
Going high up into space and falling back down to Earth,
Which sums up me!

With a loud bang and strong odour,
Party poppers are let off,
Colourful string goes over the floor,
Pink, yellow, red and blue
What more could you ask for?

Joyfulness is happiness,
While joy can be love.
The butterflies keep chasing
And the last we see, a white dove.

Michaela Silvester (14)
Prior's Field School

Carousel

The Carousel of Emotions
A swirling whirlwind, out of control
Thoughts and feelings all interwoven
As the horses go up and down

High we rose into the golden sky
Where happiness greeted us with a smile
And everything was good and everything was beautiful -
The sweetness of joy, the touch of delight.

But then we descended deep into sadness
And all the greatness disappeared, as
Bitter memories were brought back to life
Opening the gates for tears.

Up again, and then it was love
Simple, but yet so complicated
The scent of wine-red roses in bloom,
The ramblings of old romantic songs.

Next it was anger, boiling, red-hot
Rivers of rage pulsing through my veins
Huge overflows of pent-up frustration
Screams and cries that will not stop.

And then, the most terrifying of all
Its rusted chains bind and hold,
Sometimes for a day, sometimes for a life:
The never-ending caverns of despair.

And lastly, hope, pure and magnificent
The blessed knowledge that something good shall come;
When it finds you, welcome it with open arms
For it is the strongest of all the emotions.

But what I realised as the carousel ride went on
Was that I was not alone, for
While I rode through the highs and lows of life
Other people were living them too.

We all cried and hurt and loved
We all fought and felt and lived
We all smiled the most wonderful smiles
We all heard the same music as the carousel twirled.

The Carousel of Emotions
A swirling whirlwind, out of control
Thoughts and feelings all interwoven
Watch me take them in my stride . . .

Annabel James (13)
Prior's Field School

Jealousy

Green ivy creeping up your skin,
Coiling itself,
Working up from your toes,
Cutting off your windpipe
And suffocating you.
Slowly it tightens itself,
Closing you off from everything and everyone,
Eventually killing you.

The desire for something,
Your fingertips ache and go green,
It seems as though
You're giving off steam,
You're standing still,
Everything blurry
All around you,
Closing in.

You grow old and tired
From many sleepless nights,
Just staring at the stars.
You're lonely and trapped,
Suffocated and sad,
Angry and frustrated,
But most of all
Jealous.

Sophie Dangerfield (13)
Prior's Field School

Horror

The Thornbush Woods,
Where my sisters and I played,
Destroyed by a storm.
Now, all dead it lies, with,
Lightning-struck trees.
The once existent path now gone.
Hidden beneath a carpet of dead leaves.

But these things I hardly notice,
As we draw near to our special clearing.
A private place,
Where the fairies dance,
On a moonlit night.
(That's what we think,
Grown-ups just think it is silly nonsense).

In the clearing we had drawn a circle,
Into the very earth itself.
Our magic circle.
In this now lies . . .
Lucy,
My sister.
Dead, crushed by a tree!

I feel the colour drain from my face.
I can't believe it,
I won't believe what I'm seeing.
I begin to shake.

My younger sister, Julie,
Stands beside me.
But I don't notice her now.
I only remember she's there when

I hear her gulp, then sniff.
I turn slowly,
To face her.
With the awful truth.

She's as white as a ghost,
Crying silently.
Her eyes are wide with shock,
Her face a mask of horror.
Julie?
I slowly take her hand in mine,
Cold as ice.

The Thornbush Woods,
Where my sister and I play.
Destroyed by a storm,
With them,
My sister,
Lucy.

Hannah Perrin (13)
Prior's Field School

Mystery

Once upon a midnight clear
Where no sound could be heard
Above the hills
And no movement could be seen

A howling of a dog was heard
In a little girl's dream

The little girl went walking
She could still hear the scream
Of the dog in the wood
That no one could see

Suddenly the trees started creaking
It seemed the forest was speaking
There was a glimpse of her mother
In the mist

Then the howling was gone
The morning came upon her
With the dawn.

Laura Little (11)
Prior's Field School

My Best Friend

I love to know when I draw near,
My faithful friend will soon appear,
Not expecting any praise,
Not to wile away the days,
Just because she wants to say,
'Hello,' 'How are you?' and 'Good day.'
I love to see that wagging tail,
To greet me she will never fail.

I love to know she cares for me,
By the way her head rests on my knee,
The way she'd never growl or bite,
She doesn't have one drop of spite.
To say she's flawless would be wrong,
My love for her will still be strong,
Good traits abound, they're plain to see,
Her faults, they do not trouble me.

It is unquestionable to say,
Our friendship's not just for one day
And that we are the best of friends,
Forever and beyond the end.

Joanna Moore (12)
Prior's Field School

The Owl

Every night the barn owl waits
Standing like a sentry
Huge eyes staring in the dark
Waiting . . .

Every night the barn owl swoops
Looking for his supper
Razor claws searching the ground
Killing . . .

Molly Williams (11)
Prior's Field School

Abandoned

Far down a narrow lane I lie
Big, empty eyes look to the sky
Bruised, bent and battered on all sides

It happened many days ago
My owners said I had to go
What lay ahead I did not know

I was born in '63
In Dagenham far from the sea
Ford Cortina marked on me

Fly-tipped was I in this lay-by
Under a dark and inky sky
My driver did not say goodbye

My tyres were snatched, my paint's been scratched
Boot emptied and all seats were slashed
My windows and my lights were smashed

And now I wait in misery
For someone to set fire to me
And then my soul will be set free!

Alice Moore (12)
Prior's Field School

Freedom

I know of a place,
Where the sky meets the ground.
An endless blue stretches overhead,
An empty azure dome, full of dreams.
Sunlight, like liquid gold on the snow,
Warming me with its gentle kiss.
Where clouds are few; tiny white sails,
The feather moon floats high in the morning.
The crisp, cold air holds a wild tang
And an eagle soars,
With freedom under its wings.

Zoë Hackett (12)
Prior's Field School

The Leaves Are Falling Down

The leaves are falling down,
Right straight onto the ground,
With a flitter and a flutter,
They are all around.

The leaves are falling down,
When nobody's around,
Swiftly, smoothly, silently
Then they touch the ground.

The leaves are falling down,
Without a single sound,
They fly through the air and float,
Gently to the ground.

The leaves have fallen down
They are scattered on the ground
Abandoned their tree forever
Until the next time around.

Anna Wilkinson (12)
Prior's Field School

November

Dewdrops glistening,
Fog enclosing,
Footsteps crunching,
Laughter floating,
Rockets bursting,
Smoke invading,
Bonfire crackling,
Sparklers sparkling,
Guy Fawkes burning,
Bright lights gleaming,
Families celebrating,
Winds are whistling,
Treetops rustling,
This is November.

Karis Hole (12)
Prior's Field School

Listening In The Corner

A happy photo, all smiles - no worries
Mum putting my hair into bunches
Dad reading the newspaper
One big happy family, family, a family as one

Times go by; autumn stretches into winter
Emotions run high and I look outside
White, grey and brown
All I can hear is shouting - both of them . . . at each other
As I sit huddled in the corner listening, listening,
listening once more.

Sister wailing when shouts turn into bellows
Neither Mum nor Dad turns to look
Instead they let us watch and hear
My whole world collapses before me
As I sit huddled in the corner listening, listening,
listening once more.

It carries on day after day
Christmas turkey eaten in silence
Gulp - chew - gulp - chew
Presents left unopened - no cookies left for Santa
No one speaks as I sit huddled in the corner listening,
listening, listening once more.

Dad grumbles, Mum cries
He gives me and my sister cuddles -
And says nothing more except that he will see us soon
Dad picks up his suitcase and leaves us with our last
memory of the door closing.
I sit huddled in the corner crying, crying, crying of
hurt, empty and rejected.

Chantal Cox-George (12)
Prior's Field School

The Bitter Cold, Moonlit Night

It was a bitter cold, moonlit night,
with a wind that sent a chill of fear,
or could it be the black-haired girl
slowly, slowly, slowly drawing near?
For earlier on in the damp, dull day
she took her dog through the wood
but it gave an almighty tug
off came the leash
the dog ran, ran, ran.
She tried to keep up with her loyal dog
but her clumsy two legs stumbled and fell.
Down she fell into the leaves and bark
when she looked up all was dark.
She got up and looked for the path
but there was nothing to see
except the shadows of the bitter cold night.

As the black-haired girl walked on
she brushed her hair off her pale skin.
She stopped as she heard a movement in the shadows.
Her heart missed a beat,
as she drew in a short, sharp breath.

The sound drifted on
and all was silent again.

She tried calling out incase her voice was heard
but she was too scared,
she couldn't speak a word.

When after only a minute
it seemed like a year
she heard a high bark
far into the night
she looked around
her eyes shone bright.

She ran faster, faster, faster
as the barking got louder,
her hopes got higher.

She ran in and out of the moonlit trees,
the barking stopped.
There in front of her was her loyal dog lying dead
in a pool of blood shining in the moonlight.

She looked around in shock and fear,
for the time was drawing near.
Suddenly everything went black
all hopes were lost
all fears found

She turned around and ran faster, faster, faster
into the bitter cold, moonlit night.

Stephanie Wilson (11)
Prior's Field School

The Phantom

He crept into the house,
Not knowing what to do,
His body very shaken,
In the cold winter night.

He slipped through the corridor
And up the crooked stairs,
Until he found a bedroom,
With lots of doors in sight.

He picked a door quite randomly,
Still a little shaken,
For what might lie behind it,
He wasn't very sure.

The doorknob turned rapidly
And wasn't that a scare,
For inside it lay a phantom
And yet another door.

Now when you see a darkened house,
On a cold winter night,
Remember the boy who shook,
When he saw the phantom's surprise.

Jessica Martyn (11)
Prior's Field School

When The Last Leaf Falls

He said he'd be here
He said he'd call
He said he'd be waiting
For the last leaf to fall.

A long time ago
He said it last year
He said he'd be waiting
Right over here.

He might love another
He might never come
He promised he would be here
My body turned numb.

I turned and ran home
Back through the wood
I should have stayed
I knew that I should.

It wasn't my fault
He said he'd call
He said he'd be waiting
For the last leaf to fall.

Eleanor Mitchell (12)
Prior's Field School

Autumn Leaves

Orange, red and golden,
All twirling to the ground,
Touch down like a fairy,
Not even making a sound.

Pirouetting along the dusty road,
Not stopping for the cars,
Dancing furiously in the wind,
Settling down under the stars.

Louise Packer (11)
Prior's Field School

Live For The Moment

More than once or twice a day,
Either when I work or play,
I think about my living past,
Of my old school and my old class
And I wish I could return.

In nursery school when I was young,
We would play with clay, that was fun,
Drawing pictures with a finger,
Oh those memories do linger
And I wish I could return.

At primary school was my best friend,
Those memories will never end,
We'd be read a story every day
And have a video on Friday
And I wish I could return.

I made a friend at my next school,
Her name was Charlie, she was cool.
The lessons were far more grown up,
In tricky places, we'd look up
And I wish I could return.

At Prior's Field school it's a new beginning,
So much homework, my head is spinning!
And when I'm rushing to my class,
I stop to think of my time past
And I wish I could return.

And in the future, I do know,
I'll wish I were where I am now.
But I've learned that the past I must let go,
I'll enjoy the present, then I'll know,
To always live the moment.

Fiona Stewart (11)
Prior's Field School

The Very First Day Of Term

The uniform hung in the wardrobe, all smart and uncreased.
The hockey stick and tennis racquet waiting propped by the door.
The bag with all the pencils waiting to do their work.
All the new equipment waiting to be used on *the very first day of term.*

Butterflies fluttered busily in her tummy
As she went on her first journey to school
When she got there a prefect took her to the classroom.
Half nervous, half excited, she followed the prefect and took
                                        her first few steps.

The building seemed very big.
The corridors like a maze.
She tried to memorise key places.
But there was too much to take in.

At the end of the first day of term she had done a lot.
She found her way to the hall, dining hall and classroom.
She was given loads of new books for different subjects.
She had also made new friends.

She realised how much fun the day had been
And could not wait to see what the next day would bring.

Rebecca Merrick-Willson (11)
Prior's Field School

Summer

The dazzling sunshine gleams on my head,
The lovely freshness of the clear water,
Oh, what a beautiful summer's day.

No clouds in the sky,
Not much dew on the grass,
Oh, what a beautiful summer's day.

The sky is turquoise,
The flowers are delightful,
Oh, what a beautiful summer's day.

Louisa Boersma (12)
Prior's Field School

Horses

The wild horses that explore the lands
Their hooves that thunder on the ground
Their flowing black manes whisk in the air
They whistle and whinny, neigh and snort
They have wild, black eyes that shimmer with light
They rear and buck, flicking their hooves
They paw the ground angry and fierce
They flick their tails at the flies
And chomp the lush green grass.
They're ready, ready to fight for their lives
To be caught by creatures worse than lions
Humans.
Humans ride them hard and strong
Hitting them with pieces of leather
However much the horses try
They cannot get rid of these creatures.
Many are put into slavery
Pulling and pulling, heaving and heaving
Struggling with that heavy load
Never again will they be free
This is the end for these beautiful creatures.

Emily-Mei Cross (12)
Prior's Field School

The Cat

Silently, slowly creeping past,
'I've just had a sleep - don't mind me.
I found your bed very comfortable.
What am I having for dinner?

I've had salmon for breakfast and lunch,
So surely I need something to crunch!
Time for a prowl. Who's out there?
Maybe I'll find my own dinner to munch.'

Rachel Harrison (12)
Prior's Field School

Cats In Winter

A creamy body against the snow,
He was once so white but is now not so.

He lifts each paw and gives them a shake,
'What is this stuff and why is it late?'

Now for the ultimate test!
Will he get out of this awful mess?

Slipping and sliding across the ice,
This is the part that is not so nice!

Back on the snow he regains his pose,
Then a snowflake lands on his nose!

He trots back up to the house he loves,
Once inside he is as white as a dove.

He starts to nestle next to the fire,
There you go, my little sire.

Bella Cuthbert (12)
Prior's Field School

My Sister's Leaving

My sister's leaving me, what am I going to do?
I don't want her to leave. I don't know what I should do,
I think I would run around the place tearing out my hair,
Wondering when she would be back.

My sister's leaving, leaving, leaving - she's leaving me today.

I didn't like what I saw,
Packing her bags convinced me that it was really true,
She looked at me and turned away, what was she going to do?

My sister's leaving, leaving, leaving - she's leaving me today.

She's packed and leaving, it's all really true,
She's running, running to the train,
I can't believe my eyes.

My sister has left, left, - she has left me for good.

Isobel Breen (11)
Prior's Field School

Map Mysteries

Here lies the tale of my journal
I set sail towards the island
which my map described.
To find my grandfather's fortune
There was a mist ahead hovering
under the jewelled sky.

Bless those who travelled with me
through gales and through storms.
The strong scent of salt wash was unbearable
to those who came closest.
There was a mist ahead hovering
under the jewelled sky.

Through the waves we sailed south;
south west, south east wondering what
the fortune would be.
Up deck, down deck wondering what
the fortune might be.
There was a mist ahead hovering
under the jewelled sky.

We arrived at the island and took a glance
around to check that there were no pirates
but we could not hear a sound
We thought it was deserted but . . .
There was a mist ahead hovering
under the jewelled sky.

There was a mist ahead in broad daylight
and no treasure to be found
but five long-lost souls.
Now a shadow of darkness
And that's how the story's told.

Charlotte Smith (11)
Prior's Field School

A Child's Nightmare

There was a child in a school, he was the worst of them all,
Once he got told off and sent to the head,
He stayed there for a very long time,
The kids in the school saw his image,
In the tower window he was
Crying,
Crying and crying evermore.

The other kids whimpered to see him there all alone,
The child kept on crying, crying and crying on and on.
They thought we have to help him,
So that night on they crept to save the boy they loved so much.
Who just kept on?
Crying,
Crying, crying evermore.

They reached the stairs which led to the forbidden tower.
They gulped and took one step,
Two, three . . . and after a while reached half-way,
Stopped and listened to the creaking coming from below,
The silent whistling flowing around the old school castle
They all felt shivers up their spines,
They heard the boy who kept on
Crying,
Crying and evermore.

There was a teacher coming,
They dashed to the sides and stood so flat,
The teacher was getting closer, closer, closer,
The teacher approached the children who ran higher then stopped
They faced the witch
(As they called her) the witch was furious and ushered them up
They reached a door, locked and sealed
The witch opened it, in there was the boy
They loved so much

He was with nothing, but a little soup and bread,
The witch threw the kids who came to rescue the boy
Into the room with him,
The children kept on
Crying,
Crying, crying evermore.

Katie Cotterell (11)
Prior's Field School

Christmas

As I lie awake in the dark of the dark night,
I hear the kitchen clock going tick-tock, tick-tock.
I look out of the window and all there is to be seen is darkness,
I start to get excited about getting up the next morning, as it is
Christmas!
As I imagine the day that lies ahead, my mind wanders fancifully.
I draw a picture in my mind of the snow
delicately landing like magic fairies around me,
The excitement creates a sharp shiver that runs down my back
at the thought of the packaged presents that lay strewn
under the towering Christmas tree,
The burning embers start to dance like ballerinas;
pop, crackle, and *snap* they splutter.
My mind wanders ahead as I can almost taste the lunch
appearing before my hungry eyes.
I get a whiff of roast turkey and the steaming broccoli.
I talk to the boring adults instead of the PlayStation.
Escaping the torture of the grown-ups,
I play outside with my obliging animals,
the snow falling, I look inside and I suddenly realise
how alive the house looks with the Christmas tree.
Sadness clouds my thoughts though,
as I think of a whole year I have to wait
until I can experience the excitement of Christmas once again.

Ruth Grundy (11)
Prior's Field School

Silver Angel

When the sun starts to set
And the moon starts to rise,
A silver angel appears out of the sky,
She starts to sing and dance as well,
She's the silver angel that I love well.

Every night when the stars appear,
A glittering angel starts to appear,
She has long, golden hair,
With streaks of blonde
And two little golden wings,
That are silver-lined bold.

I love that little fairy,
Or angel she is,
Her lovely rose flower,
That she lives in.

Her golden-brown eyes,
Her silk-lined dress,
All put together is the best,
I love her voice all timid and small,
With timid little feet just like it.

She holds a star
And eternal water as well,
For anyone who dares to try break her spell . . .

Rachinee Young (11)
Prior's Field School

Without My Mum

I try to feel all grown up,
As if I do not care,
But life's just not the same, however you look,
If my mum is not there!

I can prance around the shops
And see all kinds of clothes so *cool* . . .
. . . But on my own it's just not right
And I'm left with sisters who *rule!*

You can't do this, you can't buy that . . .
It's too expensive, don't you see.
You're still young, your time will come,
Keep up! Don't lark around with me!

Now here's a thing which bothers me,
When no mum's around to know,
Where does the money in my purse,
Just evaporate and *go?*

I like to have her gently near,
To keep me safe and sound
And know that if I'm lost and drift about,
There's always *Mum* to see I'm found.

Through thick and thin it's good to know,
My mum's so kind and fair
For when I grow old, I'll remember the days
When my mum wasn't there!

Katie Lewis (11)
Prior's Field School

New School

She entered through the big oak doors,
The school seemed like any other,
Children chatting,
Tutors teaching,
A general school atmosphere.
Classes were the same as usual,
Everything was normal - till break.

The playground was blank and lifeless,
The students seemed hard and hating.
They cut her out,
Yet said to her,
'We are told to hate you, new girl,
We are told to make you leave, now,
Leave new girl or you'll wish you had.'

She told the teachers later on,
They said they weren't surprised at all,
They told her that
She should be gone.
She had to know what it was that
Made them hate her so very much
And come to that her family.

Her parents had sent her to board,
Away, at this new and strange school.
She wrote back home,
To tell her thoughts,
And say, 'This school is hideous,
Its true name is Montague Saint!'
She signed the letter 'Capulet'.

The next day everyone seemed pleased,
They said there was a party soon,
Especially
To honour her
They seemed much nicer in a way
And seemed that they had got just what
They had expected there and then.

The party did seem quite eerie,
Though every single girl was there,
Then halfway through,
They drank a toast
And said there would be a surprise
And when they said this every girl
Struck up a smirk, upon her face.

'The time has come,' the head girl said,
'To show what this school is made of -
Bring him out, now!'
She cried with glee
And out he came, bound and tied, and
Vulnerable and innocent
And more than that, he was her dad.

She ran towards him, desperate,
Hurling first years out of the way,
She pulled the knots
And ripped the rags,
To set him free and let him go.
The head girl laughed, as did the rest,
While she left her father and ran.

She ran as far as she could go,
She speedily ran to the door,
It was locked tight,
She was locked in.
There was one other unlocked door,
But it was a high-walled bathroom
And the head girl stood there and laughed.

She threw aside the heavy door
And dashed into a cubical,
She scaled the walls,
Through a window
And down, down, down, onto the ground,
She fled from the building, running
And running, from her strange school life.

She first ran back to her dorm room,
She quickly packed her things and left.
She ran back home,
Back home again.
She was not missed or even thought about,
But she was not yet forgotten,
She was gone - not at all there.

Sophie Valentine (11)
Prior's Field School

Music

When you see the notes assembled on the blank page
Some people believe they have no meaning

But when you hear them sung or played
You wonder how you ever doubted them

Music, music, music
It makes up most of our lives
If there was no music can you imagine
What life would be like?

No music to listen to on the way to school or work
No music in shops or at home while you work.
Just silence

Just stop right now while you are reading this and
Listen . . .

I bet you can hear some kind of music.
Can you imagine it not being there?
What would we talk about when there is not much happening?

We need music to live
Life would be impossible without it!
What would you do without music?

Harriet Barnes (13)
Prior's Field School

The Lundies

As they were galloping along.
The trees were falling on the ground.
Their manes were swirling around in the cold breeze like twisters.
The forelocks were moving around the eyes.
As they annoyed them.
The stifles in their legs were working so hard
And sounded like thunderclaps.
The storm raged again.
The horses extended into a trot.
Soon they were galloping.
The anger of the storm made the leaves come off the trees.
And they were swirling around them.
They reared up into the air
as the screaming wind howled around them.
Soon . . .
They calmed down to a walk.
The wind died down again.
And the twister twirled into the distance.
As the sunset blushed at the end of the day . . .
Now they walk into the light.

Hazel Williams (12)
Prior's Field School

The Sea

The sea so big,
So calm and peaceful,
The gentle ripples
Glistening in the setting sun.

Then a big wave,
Approaching slowly from the horizon,
A splash against the shore,
And then the sea is still once more.

Maddy Gooding (12)
Prior's Field School

Panther

I see a shadow on that hill,
The red eyes pierce me, hit me and stare.
It's crawling towards me.
I am safe high above the world in my lonely universe.
My hands, sweaty and cold,
Clasp the firm handle of my only protection.
It's chasing something now . . .

It strikes!

My lethal pistol is shaking in my untrustworthy hand.
I pull the stiff trigger and hear a short, sharp *pop!*
I'm shuddering in my high tree branch.
I am like a little girl clasped in a witch's gnarled hand,
Unable to escape from what I have just done.
I had a clear view.
Autumn has passed and winter has taken its toll.
No leaves remain on the witch-like fingers.
Giving me no way of error.
The long shape of a large beast now lay on the frosted pasture.
I do not know what it is, but I know it faces no misery.
That black panther will have to find another animal to kill if it wants
Its prey live.
I see a shadow on that hill,
The red eyes pierce me, hit me and stare.

Caroline Hughes (13)
Prior's Field School

You

You saved me from a broken heart
And a dying soul,
A tired mind
And the drifting wings of my imagination,
The depression of my collapsing world
You were my saviour,
You were my hope,
You were my love.

Sophie Waller (14)
Prior's Field School

Babies

Babies are born and cry, oh they do,
They sit on the floor and spill things on you,
They make you stressed, they make you tense,
If only they were born with common sense.

They wake you up so early in the morning,
Just as the sun is waking up and dawning,
You hear a scream, you hear a cry,
You rush to their bedroom and wonder why.

They look at you with a smirk,
You pat them on the back and they do a big burp,
So you change their nappy
And they're so much happier.

Sooner or later they're walking and talking,
Phoning and texting,
Going out drinking,
They're driving me insane,
How I wish they were babies once again.

They're growing up now, going into the wild,
Hoping to get married and have a child,
Babies are born and cry, oh they do,
They sit on the floor and spill things on you . . .

Harriet Lawson (13)
Prior's Field School

The Blue Bird

The blue bird swept over the bright blue sky,
The spongy clouds way up high,
He soars in and out and up and down
Gracefully like a floating balloon,
I hope to see my blue bird soon.

Charlotte Aiken (11)
Prior's Field School

Nothing Out Of The Ordinary

It is five seconds to 10 o'clock,
you watch the hands on your watch,
five, four, three . . . and one,
brrr, the bell goes.
Nothing out of the ordinary
excited screams bounce around you,
but never aimed at you.
It is silent once again,
you look around at the simple
room that you sit in day after day,
you have been left by yourself.
Nothing out of the ordinary.
As you bend down to pick up
your books, your mind fills
with fear, who would get
you this time?
Would it be huge Harry?
Or big Ben the boxer?
Nothing out of the ordinary.
As you move towards your locker,
an uncontrollable fright rolls
through you like a clap of thunder,
it starts at the tips of your
toes and makes its way
to the ends of your hair.
Nothing out of the ordinary.
You squint, opening one eye to
who will pounce on you like
a golden lion, flipping his
mane, knowing he is the champion,
but wait, you are standing all
alone in an empty corridor,
the only noise to be heard is
the pit-pat from the drip of the tap
 . . . how strange, how out of the ordinary.

Florence Pickard Price (13)
Prior's Field School

A Homeless Man's Tribute To His Dream Lady

Every night I dream . . .
I dream of her and I together,
She makes me feel so sensational,
She has long, blonde, flowing hair
And eyes as blue as the crystal blue sea,
She will walk past me every day
And just smile and give me a swish of her hair,
I can smell her sweet scented perfume as she delicately swifts past,
Her warm, glowing smile fills me with happiness and joy,
She wears a long, white, luscious fur coat that sweeps past me,
The golden-blonde curls that gently sway from side to side,
Her big, soft, baby-pink lips that always so pout,
She has a magnificent Roman nose
That make her facial features stand out,
I don't know of her name, I never will . . .
I'll lay out here waiting for her to come one day,
I think about her and it makes me have a huge, warm smile,
All of this is in my dream
The dream I want to happen.

Amy Cooper (13)
Prior's Field School

October

October dyes the lane side leaves
And blows them with its bitter breeze
Collecting conkers is the thing
For schoolboys wanting to be 'king'
You kick your way through autumn's coat
The air is sharp - and so's your throat
The days (you find) are cutting in
Hurrah! Half term will soon begin
But will October's final whirl
Trick or treat this birthday girl?

Claire Harding (12)
Prior's Field School

Lost

Sitting still,
a gentle breeze upon my face.
I glare into the far distant
sunset.

My love is gone forever now.
No more may I see his
gentle face.
And sadder still I seem to grow,
in memory of his dark blue eyes.

A locket I hold in my grasp.
Once holding memories, now
just empty, an echoing tunnel
of misery with every glance.

For me the future is bleak,
empty, for now my grief is
beyond me and my heartache is
unbearable.

Camilla Carter-Meggs (13)
Prior's Field School

From Up Above

From up above
The balloons are drops of candyfloss
Pink like the sunset clouds

From up above
The different colours of hair
Seem so vague

But when you get down
Their clothes are torn
Like snake's skin

When you get down
The people's faces are smeared
With unhappiness.

Elizabeth Westwood (12)
Prior's Field School

My Phobia

I can see it there in the corner of my bedroom,
Waiting to pounce,
I can see its shadow on the wall,
I can feel it look at me with its beady eyes.
I can see its black body
And hairy, long legs,
And then it makes its escape,
I jump on the nearest chair
Argh . . .
It runs across the carpet,
Its legs running as fast as it possibly can under the table,
It tries to go through the crack in the wall,
But I get there first with my big foot.
Splat!
At least I won't be seeing that spider
Again . . .

Hannah Lemieux (13)
Prior's Field School

The Boy

One lonely boy sitting alone
His mother has died and he wants a home.
No one to love him and no one to care,
Crying his eyes out on his long, brown hair.
Looking around trying to find maybe just one person
Who will be so kind,
To give him some money or goods for the week
So he won't have to starve on the rations he eats.
Then comes along a man who looks nice,
Maybe he's seen him once or twice.
The man bends down and gives him one pound,
One big coin that is oh so round.
The man smiles and walks away,
He hopes he'll come back another day.

Jessica Harris (13)
Prior's Field School

Lost

Small cat, black last seen
On the 19th of September
It says in large black print.
The ink on the poster is starting to drip
Because it's raining and I am dripping wet.
This is the fifth day in a row
That I have been out here,
Screaming his name.
The tarmac is slippery,
I lose my step,
I'm on the ground,
The rain falling hard on my face,
I shut my eyes tight.
I am soaked to the skin.
I call his name,
But the only answer I get
Is the distant sound of cars.
As I open my eyes
The rain's still falling,
I try one last call
As a large tear falls down my frozen cheek.
I shut my eyes tight,
Perhaps my mummy is right.
Maybe it is time I gave up.

Jessica Trendle (12)
Prior's Field School

Dreaming Of Elephants (Haiku)

A moving mountain,
Immense, grey and beautiful,
With eyes like opals.

Erin Hackett (12)
Prior's Field School

Seasons

The garden sleeps.
All is quiet,
Frost hardening to ice,
Snow draping the trees
Turning them to a white lace, blanketing the sky.
The dark green fir of the trees
Swallows the last of the birds
But - bulbs are sleeping, waiting . . .
Trees like ghosts hang over and
frighten the last of the flowers
Until -
Spring
shoots sprouting from the soil,
Daffodils happily smile among the fresh green in the beds,
Always touched by a gentle warming breeze.
The orange and yellow of the daffodils
deeply contrast with scarlet tulips.
Lambs joyfully bounce among the fields
until they grow
in summer.
Roses like heavenly cabbages,
unearthly pinks, yellows and the deepest of all reds
scavenge through the hard, dry soil.
Trees in full bloom
like giant mushrooms
softly shade the flowers,
pom-poms of dandelions
drift to a new destination where
autumn casually draws in,
the climax of the summer turning brown,
the wind blows impetuously
dried leaves fall like cornflakes,
apples, fruit ripening,
hanging like red dimples on the tree
and behind our back the temperature falls.

The garden sleeps once more.

Sarah Bowling (12)
Prior's Field School

The Legend

So you say you are a legend,
What do you have, some special gift
Or is it you are always in with the drift?
So you say you're cool,
Do you tell people what they can and can't do?

I always thought a legend was a myth,
So you say it's not always an ancient story?
Why is there some special power?
Then you will have to be locked in a tower.

Then you won't be what you are,
You will just be one of those ancient myths
Nobody will know you or where you're from,
You'll just be one of those things on a CD-ROM
You will then be known as what you want,
You! In that tower you're a legend.

The as the years go by,
Everyone will forget you ever exist.
You'll just be one of those things in a tower,
Then you'll lose your name and everything you own,
That's when you realise what you are,
You're just nobody.

Katriona Mckinnia (13)
Prior's Field School

Calmed By The Sea

Brave little horse along the wet, sandy shore
Breathing in the morning air,
Hooves splashed by waves.

Reluctantly stares at his reflection
Calmly drags his feet,
Watches his step carefully as he walks
Further and further out of his depth.

Little horse calmed by the sea.

Georgia Brooks (11)
Prior's Field School

Christmas Time

I can't believe it is time already,
I have been waiting for it all year!

The lights twinkling on the tree,
With the presents wrapped up beautifully.

I go shopping with my friends to buy presents,
And I can't stop thinking what the receiver's face will be like
when they see it!

Dad is making mulled wine,
And making everyone have a sip.

Mum is wondering when the turkey is going to come,
And cooking her first batch of chestnuts.

My brother is making long lists of what he wants,
Most of them are useless rubbish from the toy shop.

My sister is writing a letter to Father Christmas,
And complaining that she didn't get a pony last year!

And I am listening to the Christmas No 1 hits,
Dancing around the house until I am too out of breath
to do it anymore!

Harriet Durban (12)
Prior's Field School

School Dinners

Mushy peas and pie,
Carrots, soggy chips and rice pudding,
They're all the same,
Disgusting!

Can't wait to go home,
I'll have lots of food,
(As I don't eat at school)
Mum asks what I've eaten
I say nothing at all*!*

Lauren Silvester (11)
Prior's Field School

Autumn Days

Wonderful colours
all around,
yellow, red
green and brown.
Cooling breeze
on autumn day,
trees and leaves
can't help but sway.
Little birds
make their nest,
badgers in their
tunnels rest.
Leaves fall
and crunch around,
the only place
peace is found.
Squirrels hide
their nuts in grass,
as the day
wanders past.

Kate Valentine (13)
Prior's Field School

Horse

The sound of thundering hooves
As a horse gallops across the field
She slurps up the water from the tank
It drips and she is off
She gallops through a flock of birds
And jumps over a broken log
Her friends follow her wherever,
Wherever she goes.

Charlotte Cowley (13)
Prior's Field School

The Roses

The flower of love,
In many different ways.
Forgiveness and gain,
Peace, not pain.

White roses for love,
Dead or forsaken.
White so pure,
Clear, yet no more.

Pink roses for love,
Hopeful and expectant.
Pink so sweet,
Yet not for me.

Red roses for love,
Triumphant and perfect.
Red for blood,
Red for love.

Phoebe Richards (12)
Prior's Field School

Watch The Rose

My love for you is strong, my dear,
As strong as a red rose,
Oh how I wish to be let into your world,
As you are so beautiful and fine.
Watch what happens to the rose, my love,
Because that will happen to you.
The rose will wrinkle and perish, my love
And so will your beauty too.
But if you let me into your world,
I will let you into mine.
And by doing this, my love,
For me your beauty will stay strong and fine.

Georgie Lamden (14)
Prior's Field School

The Four Seasons

The summers are hot with sunny spells,
The free birds are flying by.
People lazing on the lawn,
Staring at the turquoise-blue sky.

The autumns are cold with foggy spells,
The coloured leaves are falling by.
The birds are flying south in great flocks,
But the young birds don't quite know why!

The winters are freezing with frosty spells,
Red-nosed children running by.
The cold is cruel to the feeble birds,
Wrapping the presents with the last brightly-coloured tie!

The springs are wet with rainy spells,
The sprinkles of blossom are falling by.
The daffodils are peeping from the grass,
With the foxgloves reaching sky high!

Laura Swain (13)
Prior's Field School

Just Remember The Good Things

You may be down
And wear a frown,
But just remember the good things.

The sky may be grey
And it may rain today,
So just remember the good things.

School may be tough
And life may seem rough,
But remember the good things.

Just remember how lucky we are,
Not to be born under a dark star,
Think of all the good things you have
And life will take you far.

Camilla Eason (11)
Prior's Field School

Hallowe'en

Once a year on one dark night,
the dead people come out to fight.

The headless man and the one-eyed croan,
escape from their graves and begin to moan.

The little children are unaware,
of what's really out there.

Most children eat their sweets,
but little do they know that they're the treat!

Ghost and ghouls are everywhere,
waiting to see who they can scare.

The wind is howling, the night is chilly,
and a mother cries, 'Where's my son Billy?'

Parents beware on Hallowe'en,
or else you'll hear your children scream.

Antonia Mills (12)
Prior's Field School

The Little Mouse

Once there was a little mouse that had tiny little ears
And lived in my house under the floorboards
Behind the stair,
No one knew the mouse was there.

The only people who knew the mouse
Were my brother and me.
It tiptoed past my knee
And ran right into my mother!

My mother screamed and the mouse ran
Straight through to my uncle Dan
He ran down the stairs and out the door
And that is all I ever saw.

Georgia Dwyer (11)
Prior's Field School

My Cat Pepsi

Pepsi is my sweet little cat
She is not the sort to sit on a mat
Instead she plays football with me
And after that we sit down for tea

She thinks she is a dog
The silly little mog
She's a really cute cat deep down
I would give her a big golden crown

Sometimes she eats moss
She thinks she is the boss
She is the dog of the house
She always brings in a mouse

When it is time for her to sleep
She lies down in a fluffy heap
She takes up all my bed
She always sleeps with Ted.

Katrina Havelock (12)
Prior's Field School

Nobody Wants Her

Nobody wants her and nobody wants to care,
She has no one to hold her hand in prayer.
No one will listen and no one wants her there,
Nobody wants her in the hot summer's air.
No one will sit with her under the tree full of pears,
Nobody will go with her and play at the fair.
Nobody will scold their children when they stare and stare,
Nobody in games wants to be her partner,
She is not part of a pair.
She can't take it anymore,
She feels as though she has to stop and end it all.
Nobody will chase her as she's walking to the end of the pier,
As she falls she screams, 'It's not *fair!*'

Lucy Wootton (12)
Prior's Field School

Robin Was A Hero

Robin was a hero,
He robbed to save the poor,
He stole only from the rich
To give the poor some more.

Money, jewels and treasure
Was what he liked to take,
But food was also needed
Like bread or meat or cake.

With his gang of helpers
Some riding on their mules,
He emptied all their pockets
Of banknotes, coins and jewels.

When Robin found the poor
Who were starving in the street,
He passed out all the money
To enable them to eat.

Robin was a great man
A hero to the poor,
Robin will be back one day
To try to pinch some more.

Fiona Stannard (12)
Prior's Field School

An Autumn Day

A carpet is laid - not a sound,
As the leaves, quite dead, fall down.

The leaves so bright, so crisp,
Fall down in a clump, quite adrift.

Their fiery colours glinting in the light,
Are ablaze and fall ever so slight.

They zigzag through the autumn air,
What a sight! Just to sit and stare.

Florence Clarke (13)
Prior's Field School

Winter

The frosty mornings,
The fresh blue air,
Jack Frost has been
With his white, crisp hair.
School children running,
Warming up the car,
Scraping down the windows,
Not wanting to be late.
Jack has frosted up the windows
And remembering the date,
The first day of winter,
At the dead of night
Jack terrorises the children,
Makes their poor hearts beat
What shall he do tonight?
While he sits and thinks in his seat
Shall he frost up the windows
Or frost up the car?
Make their little cheeks go cold
So tomorrow he will travel far.

Fern Strafford-Taylor (12)
Prior's Field School

My Pony

Sugar is my pony.
She is soft and white like silk.
She loves to canter in the woods
And rolling in the mud.

Sugar is my pony.
I love her very much.
She'll be my friend forever
And I will never forget her.

Alice Briggs (11)
Prior's Field School

Winter Night

One winter night,
a big silvery moon was shining,
brightly down on the dark countryside,
so peacefully, so high.

I was walking through
a cold, sparkly, white blanket,
snow it was.

The freezing cold air,
was biting my face so hard,
that it made my nose go pale pink marshmallow.

The moon was still shining,
brightly down the dark countryside,
so peacefully, so high.

Abby Heath (11)
Prior's Field School

Summer's Night

As I stand on a summer's night
The water still and all things right
The world in peace, the silence, calm
The whole world rests within my palm.

As birds hurry back to nests amongst the spindle vine
Seeing the great light upon the water makes all things fine
As trees sway to and fro
The light goes with them, a perfect glow.

As flowers look full with pride
Their beauty has never been denied
As I stand on a summer's night
Only in my dreams are all things right.

Emily Attwooll-Jones (11)
Prior's Field School

That Ain't My Dog

That ain't my dog
That ain't my dog
That's the one with the beak
That goes squeak, squeak
So go and look again
You remember, surely you remember the one which looks like a hen
Its eyes are red
With a candle on its head
Oh surely you remember

It has some whiskers
But it never whispers
It has two horns
It only eats corn
I know it sounds funny
But it is nicer than a bunny
Oh please, oh please find my dog
Which looks like a hog.

Georgina Bricknell (11)
Prior's Field School

Baby Sister

Can't wait to see her!
my new baby sister

She's arriving today
my new baby sister

She'll lie in her pram
my new baby sister

She'll cuddle her toys
my new baby sister

Her blue eyes will stare
my new baby sister

She'll cry when she sees
her new older sister!

Jessica Bodie (11)
Prior's Field School

Shopper

There is a woman at the supermarket where I shop,
She's crazy, she's zany, she's mad.
She dances as she pushes her trolley.
She buys tons and tons of ice cream.
She must get extremely fat.
When she sees the most unfunny things,
She laughs until her face turns red
And everyone stares.
And when she pays at the till,
She kisses the cashier on both cheeks.
Yes, she's laughable, silly and weird, weird, weird!
Oh, if only she could see herself,
She'd go even redder than red,
And run out of the shop,
Waving her arms and legs.
She'd never come back.
The shop would be greed.
No more polkadot blouses,
No more opera singing,
Oh, I'm a genius!
What a great plan!
Let's film her and make her go mad.
I'll get the whole shop on to it.
Everyone will agree, and . . .
'Time to go home now.' It's Mum.
No! My plan! Oh!
There she is right now!

Megan Abbott (11)
Prior's Field School

My Pet Goblin

I have a pet goblin, his name is Billy,
And sometimes you know he can be very silly
He rattles and screams, he makes such a din
He rattles the teapots and bashes the tin.

At night he sleeps in my bedroom drawers
Sometimes he coughs and sometimes he snores
He sometimes is happy, sometimes he is mad
But what I hate most is when he's bad!

He loves to jump and play hide-and-seek
But when it's his turn to count, he looks . . . such a sneak!
He hates to be quiet and hates to run
But what he does like is to have some fun.

His colour is green with a blue-striped shirt
I hate it when he gets it covered in dirt!
He always is dirty, he never is clean
And when it is bath time he never is keen.

My goblin's called Billy, that is his name
I love my pet goblin even though he's a pain
My mum thinks that keeping a pet goblin is silly
But I don't . . . he'll always be my pet goblin called Billy!

Claire Edginton (11)
Prior's Field School

What You Asked For I Tried To Give

You asked me for a fountain; I gave you a waterfall
You asked me for a rose; I gave you a bouquet
You asked me for a story; I gave you a book
You asked me for a chocolate; I gave you Thorntons
You asked me for a lift; I gave you a car
You asked me for an apple; I gave you an orchard
You asked me for a house; I gave you a castle
You asked me for a fir tree; I gave you a forest
You asked for love; I gave you me.

Tassja Collier (13)
Prior's Field School

The Manor House

The sad, crumbling house stands alone,
Surrounded by lonely moor
No one goes there now,
Except for the howling wind
Whistling through the cracks in the walls
And the rain tapping gently on the window frame.

It was once a fine, handsome house,
Now it is no more than a ruin,
Hung with cobwebs.

Sometimes, on a windy day,
You can almost imagine
The sound of a crackling fire
And laughter, breaking the icy cold
Of the old manor house.

Jessica Macleod (13)
Prior's Field School

What Is Love?

Man
Love is when I give you a rose. No.
Love is when I give you a poem. No.

Love is when we are together. Yes.
Love is when I would die for you. Yes.

Woman
Love was when you gave me a rose. Yes.
Love was when you gave me a poem. Yes.

Love was when we were together. Yes.
Love was when you would die for me.
I agreed

And now you are gone.

Katherine Morris (13)
Prior's Field School

Christmas Holiday

Midnight strikes the clock again.
I'm waiting for the signal.
Creep downstairs and through the lounge,
Leading to the kitchen.

There, in the corner
They're all piled up,
Wanting to open them,
Don't want to wait.

Wanting to feel them,
Guess what's inside,
I think Mum's coming!
Never mind.

Running upstairs,
Back to my room,
Quick! Get to bed,
So Christmas will come.

'Wake up darling,
It's Christmas Day.
I forgot to tell you,
We're going away.'

'What? My presents!'
'Save them!'
'What? No way!'

Antoinette Hayes (12)
Prior's Field School

Love And Hate

I love your eyes, but hate how they do not see me,
I love your lips, but hate how they do not kiss me,
I love your body, but hate how it does not caress me,
I love what I see, but hate what I might find.

Olivia Newman-Young (13)
Prior's Field School

Christmas

The happy night of every year
Finally at last is here!

Down the chimney, through the door
Jolly dear old Santa Claus!

With an overloaded sack,
Swaying slowly on his back.

Dozens and dozens of brand new toys
For all good little girls and boys.

He lays them out beneath a tree
Looking very nice to see.

At last his work is all complete
He is rewarded with a treat.

Next morning all the children scream,
Waking from a special dream.

Then a voice comes loud and clear,
'See you all again next year!'

Caroline James (11)
Prior's Field School

I'm Scared, Mummy

I'm scared of the black men, Mummy.
The way they creep up the walls
And jump on my bed in the night.
They scare me, Mummy.

I'm scared of the man in the moon, Mummy.
The way it sits in the sky and spies on me,
I think he is taking my toys.
He scares me, Mummy.

I'm scared of the darkness, Mummy.
It tiptoes into my room when I'm asleep
And hides the light so I can't see.
It scares me, Mummy.

Jenny Briscoe (14)
Prior's Field School

I Do!

Do you remember his smile?
His cheery face looking up at you?
I do

Do you remember him sitting in his chair,
Reading the paper every morning?
I do

Do you remember his paintings?
Portraits and the countryside?
I do

Do you remember him polishing his car,
Then off for a spin round the block?
I do

Do you remember him on holiday,
Sitting in his caravan in the sun?
I do

Do you remember him off for a snooze,
Then back again for drinks?
I do

I remember his happy life
And you should too.

Written especially for Gramps.

Harriet Martin (12)
Prior's Field School

My Baby!

Do you have a baby like this at home?
My baby at home has soft feet like the pillows on my bed.
As she jumps on me with her gentle fingers touching me!
When I look into her eyes they sparkle like stars in the sky!
As she sleeps at night, her little eyes closed
And baby's breathing so soft!
Goodnight baby!

Mary Stephanou (11)
St Philomena's School, Carshalton

The Mysterious Woods

I gallop across the frozen waters and hear something ahead,
I stop in silence and fear . . .
I then come face to face with a shadow,
Snow trickles down the edge of a tree.
I then see a white head . . .

I wondered who was going to make the next move,
I started to move one foot,
But I stopped as I thought I knew this animal,
I had seen it long before . . .
I was about to gallop away,
But when I turned back it was gone . . .

I started to gallop across the soft snow and I tried not to
make footprints
I was then left alone in this mysterious place . . .
Had this all been happening to me or
Was it just a dream . . . ?

Zoe Meliniotis (11)
St Philomena's School, Carshalton

A Horse's Dream

My moonlight shine,
My soft, snowy glisten.
As I gallop through the forest,
Shhh! Hoof beats, *listen!*
I skid to a halt, I turn and I stare
And I see another beautiful, snowy-white mare.

She's walking towards me, then stops halfway,
Her eyes are bright on this glorious day.
She walks on again, a trot, a canter,
My head is pounding, my heart, *pitter-patter.*

We're racing each other; our muzzles nearly touch,
I look round behind me; this is all a bit much!
I turn slowly back, not daring to look . . .
But she's suddenly gone, like the closing of a book.

Anna Desborough (12)
St Philomena's School, Carshalton

Motives

Accelerate your mind,
to a level of consciousness.
Ignore the surrounding noises
and concentrate on the sky.
Just think about it.
Don't worry.
It will all be OK tomorrow.
Let go of your troubles
and imagine a world without destruction.
A desolation of broken bricks
that never existed.
Reverse out of this world of fascination
gaze in astonishment
let go of all your tensions.
And don't worry about the neglect.
Watch as the familiar shadows slowly disappear
and a new illustration enters your head
don't let the authority bring you down
or your hallowed body
that has rearranged your mind.
Smuggle in the missing pieces
and realise the impression of life.
Don't let it cheat you out of money
don't let it disturb your operation
suggest a pinch of joy
and respond with a dash of hate.

Emily Dowler (14)
St Philomena's School, Carshalton

The Angel

Robes flowing like water,
Soft as silk, white as pearl.
Skin as cold as ice,
Pale as the moon, dry like plaster.
Hair like spun gold,
Loose curls like twisted branches.
Eyes like aquamarine stones,
Clear as diamonds, hypnotising as a vortex.
Wings like a dove,
Peaceful and powerful.
Sitting on a fluffy cloud,
Playing a golden harp.
And she called herself
Angelina the angel.

Jessica Lee (11)
St Philomena's School, Carshalton

My Cat

I can never forget the days
When I played with my cat.
Alone by the large rays,
Of the rising sun.

She was bound to me
And I to her.
All till that day
When she ran away.

I chased her, in front she looked like a dot.
But a farmer got there first.
I heard the gunshot,
Knowing it could mean only one thing . . .

Madi Barwick (11)
St Philomena's School, Carshalton

Waiting!

10.01
I was waiting, scared and frightened
Drills here and screams there,
I was waiting for braces,
All I wanted to do was run away,
Scream the place down; make a flood of tears,
So that I wouldn't await the pain that was yet
To come.

10.03
It has only been two minutes,
It's driving me insane! It really is.
Slowly and loudly drills louder and louder
I wanted to bite my nails until nothing was left but my bare skin.

10.05
Knocking and banging trying to put my teeth back into place.
Suddenly the door opens and the dentist calls my name, 'Maria.'

Maria Brooks (11)
St Philomena's School, Carshalton

Help

Creep, creep, who goes there?
Swish, swish, who was that?
Are you a ghost? Are you a man?
Are you lost? Or out to scare?
Will you go *boo?* Will I cry, 'Argh?'
Will you let me free? Or catch me in a snare?
What do I do? Who are you?
Do you know me?
Because if you do come and help me,
Please come, set me free.
Come set me free from this cold, dark place.
Come take me home, give me ice cream and cake,
Give me a hug and share some love.
Because I'm all alone, in this cold, dark, lonely place.

Rhiannon Darcy (14)
St Philomena's School, Carshalton

My Family

First is Bapa who was born in Wales,
He was in the Second World War and has many tales,
He doesn't have much hair and isn't very tall,
But we don't care because Bapa is so cool!

Lita is quite short too, quite a bit shorter than Bapa
And whenever I ring it seems that she's always making supper.
Lita is a cheerful person who never has a frown,
She likes her afternoon tea while watching Countdown.

Mama Hourie is very glamorous and likes sparkly things,
She is very fond of diamonds and has plenty in her rings.
Baba Basog loves to swim and lives in LA,
He loves it there as it's very hot and he can swim every day.

My dad is very sporty and plays basketball,
He plays in a team where they're all about four foot tall!
Dad works very hard and has done very well for himself,
By doing this he has made a lot of wealth.

My mum's two favourite things in life are chocolate and white wine,
While eating and drinking these two things, she loves to party
and dine.
She loves to dance and loves to sing,
My trendy, hip mum loves everything!

My sister Roxanna is outgoing and fun,
She loves to get a tan in the sun,
With everything Roxanna does she always tries her best,
She is the best sister in all the world I think she deserves a rest.

My other sister Rebecca loves animals and sport,
When she plays netball she runs as quick as a flash round the court.
Her riding skills are brill
And having her as a sister is a thrill.

Now you know my family,
Well, everyone except for me.

Jessica Kharrazi (11)
St Teresa's School, Effingham

The Outsider

He walks alone in the streets,
Avoided by everyone he meets.
Sits on a bench beside the park,
Waiting there till gone dark.

He sleeps beneath the stars at night,
Cold and lonely and full of fright.
A doorway is his home tonight,
Lost and lonely, a sorrowful sight.

As dawn breaks and a new day begins,
The outsider thinks of warm and special things.
He has carried his life in plastic bags,
The clothes he wears are only rags.

The outsider, we think is a lonely man,
But he lives his life as only he can.

Jessica Burgess (12)
St Teresa's School, Effingham

My Family

Firstly I will begin with my cat Buster,
he may be friendly now, but if he is angry,
he'll *scratch, scratch, scratch!*

There's also my mum and dad,
who drink tea by the litre!
They have it in the morning and evening too, *pop!*

I have two sisters called Flora and Ivy.
Ivy is always ill, Flora is always *annoying!*

Then there is me,
the cat feeder,
the tea maker,
the oldest.

Sophie Morgan (12)
St Teresa's School, Effingham

Me, Myself And I

Never have I wept when pain has bothered me
Unless it's too great to bear
But my weak, broken heart that shall never be healed
By cause of a family breakdown
That came and went.

Me, the solitary whisper of wind
That had a friend that slipped away
Now a loner in need of a friend
For the happy child to return
Again.

I still am there under the black cloud
Just in need to surface from the storm
But still I'll just wait that little longer
Then I'll come and be happy again.

Jacqueline Hedge (11)
St Teresa's School, Effingham

The Outsider

He lurks alone ostracised in the dark
Not a friend in the world
His broad figure almost monstrous
Blocks the sun from showing his hideous face

It is silent around him, bitter and damp
The adults will stare and gossip
And the children will point and shout
He remains alone, motionless, still

In the darkness that consumes his heart and his all.
Do not let his façade mislead you
He is still one of us
His strong exterior hides his emotional heart.

Emily Gray (12)
St Teresa's School, Effingham

My Family

My family is quite normal
But in many different ways
They are happy, giving and very kind too
And what awaits them, come what may

My mum is very kind
And organises lots of things to do
Like inviting people round, having fun
Oh and so many things!
My mum's nickname is Mandymoo.

My dad is very busy, but still has time for us
Her works and works and works and works
And sometimes if he's very late
It could almost be at dusk!

My dog Pepsi,
Well, what can I say?
She's a gorgeous, black, sweet and cuddly Labrador
And even goes outside on a rainy or snowy day!

My family is the best
And always will be.
And I will always, always
Remember that!

Hannah Gale (12)
St Teresa's School, Effingham

My Family

My mum, my dad and me,
This is my family.
We are as happy as can be,
My mum, my dad and me.

We have a dog called Toby,
My mum, my dad and me.
And last week I got a new puppy,
My mum, my dad and me.

We're looking forward to the holidays,
My mum, my dad and me.
When we can get away,
My mum, my dad and me.

Maybe we'll go to Spain,
Or maybe Italy.
I think it's America,
Across the Atlantic Sea.

So as you can see,
My mum, my dad and me.
Are as happy as can be,
My mum, my dad and me.

Lucy Weinreb (11)
St Teresa's School, Effingham

The Monster

The clank on the windows the creak on the floor
The shout of a person who saw the monster on the floor.

He awakens at night and sleeps in the day
Because he is so ugly they shout and throw him away.

He lives in the forest in an old and dusty shed
With the animals all around him, even on his bed.

When the sun starts to come up he knows his time has gone
And waits in his sleep for another night to come along.

Stephanie Griffiths (12)
St Teresa's School, Effingham

The Monster . . .

The monster is ugly, the monster is mean,
The monster is hideous and never is clean.
He lives in the forest and is always covered in mud
And he has always wanted to love.
His creator is Frankenstein who is very mad,
He made me look so bad.
The monster is brave, but not afraid.
He is as tall as a tree
And he loves to play with bees.
He is as tough as a rock
And he's left like an outsider
He lives in a cave
And is never afraid.
He has always wanted to love,
He would never hurt a dove.
And he sits by the lake,
Like it's no one.

Hannah Gazzard (12)
St Teresa's School, Effingham

Families

Mums, dads, brothers and sisters,
Survive the tornadoes and the blisters.

Mums want everything crystal clean,
To be neat and tidy and to be seen.

Dads are as lazy as can be,
But they're useful to pay the fees.

Brothers are sweet and annoying too
And their favourite colour is always blue.

Sisters drive you round the bend,
So you might be soon on the mend.

So all in all, families are *weird!*
But hey, at least my sister hasn't grown a beard!

Georgia Smyth (11)
St Teresa's School, Effingham

Husky In The Winter

They're grey and white
Like the gentle snow,
The husky is near
Now we must go.

The soft blue eyes
Like the crystal of the lake
The warmth and comfort
Of the husky's small face.

Suddenly I awoke
It was only a dream
But it is Christmas Day
Winter is fully here.

I ran downstairs
To see what I got
With the family waiting
With a special little box.

I opened my present first
And you'll never guess what,
A small little animal was in this box
With bright blue shimmering eyes
And fur like frost.

Charlotte Guiton (12)
St Teresa's School, Effingham

I Heard . . .

I heard the blink of an eye
I heard a spider spinning a web
I heard the heart of a human beat
I heard the roots of a plant growing underground
I heard the yawn of a hippo a mile away
I heard all of these in my dreams.

Claudia Medina-Moralejo (11)
St Teresa's School, Effingham

Life

My life is but a teardrop,
Fallen from a lonely eye,
What is the meaning of this teardrop?
That is the form in which we cry.

I am but an emptiness,
Into which we stare,
Big, black and horrific,
Almost as if a nightmare.

My thoughts and feelings but a shadow,
Reflecting my inner self,
I must not be so greedy,
Not everything is wealth.

My heart has grown old,
As so the manner in which I see -
Has become somewhat tainted,
In a world reflecting the dark in me.

This world a mirror,
Which tells me the truth,
It may hurt a little,
But makes me search for proof.

I don't care for anything more,
I am just someone sitting on the settee.
Who thinks about life,
Who thinks about me.

Hannah Lipinski (12)
St Teresa's School, Effingham

Monster

The monster rose from his shadowy bed,
Scars all over his face.
Frankenstein called him ugly,
Not possibly part of the human race.

'You are,' Frankenstein commented,
'Not quite what I expected.
In fact, I really don't like you,
So therefore you are rejected.'

The monster roared a mighty roar
And beat his bloodstained chest,
Frankie cried, 'I take back what I said,
You simply are the best!'

The monster grunted, then stormed off,
We hope, in search of food.
Though maybe it would eat a child,
Or a dog (or a really cool dude!)

'Oh no,' Frankie called out in fear,
'I've created a monster who kills.
Now it'll cost me all the damage -
Just think of all those bills!'

But then Frankenstein had a thought,
'He takes up so much space,
I'll take him up to Timbuktu,
Or perhaps another place.'

So that's just what Frankenstein did,
He thought his idea was brill,
But in the end it turned out
That the monster did nothing but kill!

Holly Baker (12)
St Teresa's School, Effingham

Autumn

Dry, crispy brown leaves,
Sprinkle down like flour,
Leaves crunching under my feet,
As I walk along dreaming.

The bare trees,
The crisp breeze,
The chilly nights,
The warm air,
As I sit in comfort, next to the fire.

The colours of the trees,
The cold blue sky,
With the sun shining down on me
As I wander in and out
Of the shadows of the tall trees.

Alice Di Mond (11)
St Teresa's School, Effingham

Tiger

A dark shape hides,
Its bright searchlight skin blinds the trees,
The tiger's emerald eyes blink,
Its long tail swishes in the wind,
The tiger's teeth glisten like diamonds,
He's hungry.

Suddenly some eyes spot a distant figure,
Paws start to move,
Stampeding faster and faster,
Claws clench hard,
Eating, eating as the dark night carries on.

Georgina Kelly (11)
St Teresa's School, Effingham

Her

She sits alone
Eating a sandwich
Which smells funky
And looks disgusting.

Her skin is greasy and covered in spots,
Her dark blue eyes
Water when she glances at us,
Her black hair shines.

Loneliness crawls along her spine
And we laugh at her aimless cries.
PE is when she's humiliated,
Drama is when she's singled out.

We look upon her as a nerd,
Only because she writes during break,
Her skinny fingers shake with fear,
As the tomboy walks her way.

But when I look at her I feel sorry,
She looks different,
Likes and does different things,
Is this why she's an outsider?

I watched her walk home once,
She was crying,
Then she fell,
Everyone saw her,
No one helps outsiders but me.

Jenni Annis (12)
St Teresa's School, Effingham

Down And Out

Seeing his reflection in the water,
Unkempt, untidy, dark and damp,
Living in a box, the world of a tramp,
Eyes that are dull, empty and cold,
Family and friends, memories that fade.

Thoughts of childhood playing in an arcade,
Summer days in the woods, heat and haze,
Camps, adventure, they all drift to the past,
The winter is long when you live outside,
Wishing for the warmth of someone else's eyes.

Roaming from place to place,
Underground tunnels, benches and parks,
Everybody so busy, always in a rush,
What's so important? What's the panic?
Shouldn't we stop? Shouldn't we think?
From a tramp's perspective you can't help but sink.

Lauren Hewett (12)
St Teresa's School, Effingham

I Remember

I remember the pain of the Second World War.
I remember when it was announced that Germany had lost the war.
I remember fighting,
I remember that day when suffering and world conflict was over,
But I was wrong.

Another war had soon begun,
It started in two thousand and three,
When America and England declared war on Iraq.

I remember seeing my children's children going out to fight,
I remember their faces and their charm,
That is all I will ever know them by, now.

Elizabeth Irvine (13)
St Teresa's School, Effingham

Down By The Lake

Down by the lake
He sits just watching
No one loves him
No one helps him
He has no friends
But yet no enemies
He sings a song
To keep him company
Down by the lake
He'll hide in trees
No one knows he's there
But I
He eats from the bins
He drinks from a fountain
But still no one cares
When the park is empty
He wanders in and out
On benches, trees and slides
When one night he climbed the rocky hill
His torn hood fell back in the wind
His hair shiny, yet tangled
His skin dirty and cut
His muddy shoes were old and worn out
He just leant forward, let go of all he held
And he was gone!

Frankie Hughes (13)
St Teresa's School, Effingham

Fragments

Look closer;
Beyond the staggering build
Of the rusted soul
Who lurches past well-to-do people
So that even they may show
A resonating pang
Of sharp-edged guilt.

In, through eyes
Jagged at the corners.
Eyes, immovable from their solemn stare
That has haunted them for such a time.
Turning down dark corridors,
Laced with cobwebs.
Not the silver, silky creations,
But the grey dust traps that are
So common in abandoned interiors.

A sudden sideways spasm
Sweeps you on your feet
And a small black door forms in front.
No handle or knocker defines it clearly to be a door.
It could just as easily be another section
Of the dusty, black wall.
But, through this door is where they lie -
The fragments.

Sharp imperfections, crooked and poorly crafted -
Yet so pure.
If only it were possible to determine how they pieced together,
Then you could save that soul and others like him.
The soul that, although wilted now, is just a boy.
But, alas, the fragments never are that easy to put together.

Daniel Alexander Howell (15)
Therfield School